ABOUT THE AUTHOR

Peter Jones started professional life as a particularly rubbish graphic designer, followed by a stint as a mediocre petrol pump attendant. After that he got embroiled in the murky world of credit card banking. Fun times.

Nowadays, Peter spends his days writing, or talking about writing.

He is the author of several popular self-help books on the subjects of happiness, staying slim and dating. If you're overweight, lonely, or unhappy – he's your guy.

He's *also* written three novels; a Rom-Com (Romantic Comedy), A Crim-Com (Crime Comedy), and a Rom-Com-Ding-Dong. He's currently working on his fourth novel, which - if it's a musical - he'll no doubt describe as a Rom-Com-Sing-Song. (Spoiler: It isn't).

Peter doesn't own a large departmental store and probably isn't the same guy you've seen on the TV show Dragons' Den

ALSO BY PETER JONES

NON-FICTION

How To Do Everything And Be Happy

How To Eat Loads And Lose Weight

How To Be Even More Attractive

FICTION

The Good Guy's Guide To Getting The Girl

The Truth About This Charming Man

My Girlfriend's Perfect Ex-Boyfriend

Start the next chapter of your life

Having been in the dating industry for many years I always get excited to read any material that will help the many singletons find love, this book gave an excellent true picture of internet dating. More importantly it gave an insight from the male perspective, which as a woman was very encouraging, his observations would be useful for men that struggle with self confidence too.

There was real laugh out moments too, Peter has a natural flair for writing with wit and integrity.

If you have recently become single through divorce, separation or partner loss and unsure of how to find a new partner this book will softly guide you through the process. He has also touched on alternative methods of dating, it will be up to you to decide which path you choose, whatever avenue you choose you will find success if you follow his hints & Tips.

So Stop Waiting & Start Dating ... Good Luck

Teresa

Really helpful guide to Online Dating!

This is a brilliantly well written, witty and amusing book which will guide you through the quagmire of online dating. It takes you through how to find a good dating site, how to set up your profile, how to avoid the nutters and how to handle the first two or three dates. Going on dates after reading this book would feel like the author's holding your hand throughout, or if threesomes aren't your thing perhaps imagine he's sitting at a nearby table smiling and nodding encouragingly at you.

The book is mostly concerned with online dating but there are good tips for speed dating, finding 'potentials' through social media etc. Definitely recommended if you are actively looking for a partner, or if you want to be actively looking but have been too scared or daunted by the prospect.

A Reader

A dating book that actually works!

This book is far more comprehensive and readable than a lot of books on dating. It is packed with so many hints and tips, do's and don'ts, all written in a really lovely chatty and often quite funny way. This book points out all sorts of things that I hadn't even thought of. Seems that the 'rules' have changed a bit since I was last single!

It is a step by step guide with Action Points along the way which really worked for me. It got me online, helped me filter out some scammers right away and get me chatting to a couple of really nice guys, I'm meeting one for coffee at the weekend!! Okay he may not be 'the one' but I have the confidence to go and find out and if not keep looking.

Would certainly recommend this book to anyone who is single and looking for Love.

(I got this book after being given the companion guide that goes with it and would highly recommend that too. It's all about making the most of yourself and it's just as reader friendly as this one.)

Reader

Learn How To Get Success With This New Book

If you are looking for your soul mate and have previously been unsuccessful this `How To' book has comprehensive advice including using On-line Dating sites.

Again Peter's book is really well laid out, with clear instructions. With a comprehensive Index it's easy to read and easy to understand, easy to dip into and easy to check certain circumstances. And there are a number of sections grouped as Action Points so you can check you're on the right road to finally find success.

Book Lover

Read more 5-star reviews at amazon.co.uk

and also at

HowToStopWaitingAndStartDating.com

How To Stop Waiting And Start Dating

Your Heartbreak-Free Guide To Finding Love, Lust Or Romance NOW!

Peter Jones

soundhaven books

Second Edition.
Published 2018, in Great Britain,
by soundhaven books
http://www.soundhavenbooks.com

First edition published in 2014 under the title
How To Start Dating and Stop Waiting

British Cataloguing Publication data:
A catalogue record of this book is available from
the British Library

This book is also available as an ebook.
The first edition is available in audio from
audible.com

Visit
www.HowToStopWaitingAndStartDating.com
for other similar books, & to contact the author.

To Jules
– my 'Top Assistant' –
who could have easily have written this guide herself.

And also to Valerie,
who is living proof that the stuff in this book
actually works.

With love & heartfelt thanks
to both of you.

xx

Best wishes

CONTENTS

TO BEGIN WITH...

On my thirty-second birthday, as I sat at my mother's dining room table in front of a large cake, thirty two candles threatening to ignite my beard should I lean too far forward, I realised that the only ambition I had left in life – the only dream I hadn't given up on – was to be married.

Or at least in some sort of steady, loving relationship.

A long term partnership with someone whose ying was a close match to my less than melodic yang.

But even this, this last naive expectation of life, was looking increasingly unlikely. Every candle on that cake was some sort of burning epitaph to just how utterly rubbish I was when it came to affairs of the heart.

There had been 'relationships' – of course there had – but I'd kind of 'fallen into them', by accident. And after the ladies in question had tried, and failed, to mould me into the kind of man they actually wanted, those relationships had withered and died. There hadn't been an 'accidental relationship' for a while. Colleagues no longer described me as an eligible bachelor. Some had started to question my sexuality.

So as my family launched into a rendition of 'Happy Birthday' I decided there and then that the prospect of being single for the rest of my days was unacceptable.

Something had to be done.

Around that time there was a BBC TV show called 'Would Like to Meet' where a team of experts (a flirt coach, an actor, and an image consultant) would take some hapless individual and turn them into a heartthrob or a man-magnet. It very quickly became my favourite TV show. I'd watch it avidly from one week to the next hoping to pick up some tips. And the conclusion I came to was that I too could do with a similar makeover – albeit without the entire viewing nation of the United Kingdom looking on.

So over the next few weeks I tracked down an Image Consultant, an actor, and finally… a flirt coach.

These days, you can barely move for self-styled relationship experts and flirt coaches – heck, I'm just about to tell you why I'm one of them – but back in 2003 I could find just one. And she ran courses.

I took several hundred pounds from my savings, and booked myself on a 'flirting weekend'. Nervously, I took my place in the front row, and when instructed I turned and introduced myself to the stunning blonde sitting next to me.

"I'm Peter," I said.

"I'm Kate," said the blonde.

Then she smiled.

And I was smitten.

The course wasn't that much of a success, in that it didn't teach me how to flirt. Not that it mattered. My strategy had worked, somewhat differently but infinitely better than I'd hoped. On the Monday evening Kate and I had our first date. By the Tuesday I'd officially found myself a girlfriend. A few months later I found myself on one knee. And a year to the day after we'd first met, I found myself married.

It didn't last.

Two and a bit years later I lost Kate. To a brain hemorrhage. At Stanstead airport.

And when the dust settled – when I adjusted to a world without my wife – I was single again. The loneliness returned. And though I'll never be able to replace my beautiful blonde, I needed to fill the space that she'd left.

Something had to be done

It's my considered belief that 'dating' – whether that be online dating, speed-dating, "hey – what's a nice girl like you doing in a place like this?" dating – is similar to job hunting; it's just as brutal, many times more frustrating, and potentially far more heartbreaking.

And just like job hunting nobody wants to become 'good' at dating. To get good you have to do lots of it, and the very fact that you have to apply for a lot of jobs – or go on a lot of dates – raises more questions than it answers. It's not really something you want to shout about. Never the less, I was determined. There was no way I wanted to return to the way things were, before Kate, life's just too damn short. So date I did.

Many, many, many times.

And finally, after a lifetime of being completely useless at finding romance, I cracked it.

There's love in my life again.

Just as there can be in yours.

Welcome to *How Stop Waiting And Start Dating.*

If you've been sitting around, on your own, telling yourself you should really make an effort and 'get out there', this book might be for you.

If you're already dating – or you've tried it – and you've encountered nothing but liars and Lotharios, started your own personal collection of dating disaster stories, all whilst beating off people you wouldn't normally look twice at, this book is probably for you.

And if you'd rather fast forward through the dating stage as quickly as possible, and find someone you'd like to have a relationship with – whatever type of relationship that might be – this book is most definitely for you.

But before you get too excited, let's establish some ground rules. Buckle up and prepare to learn the hardest lesson this book has to give.

Dating Is Tough

Like most things in life, dating isn't quite as straightforward as it first appears.

You probably know that already. Perhaps it's why you picked this book up in the first place – so it'll be of no surprise to you when I say that for every person who signs up to a dating website, or downloads a dating app, or books themselves on a speed dating event, or nervously stands before a mirror and debates the merits of one outfit over another, someone else is deleting their dating profile in a flurry of 'I'm never going to do 'that' again', swiping left continuously, or arriving home from a date, dejected and disillusioned.

So let me ask you this:

WHAT DO YOU WANT?

We'll come back to this question again in a moment, but for now I'm going to assume you want to meet someone nice? Someone you enjoy spending time with? Perhaps even someone you can potentially spend the rest of your life with?

Or do you – and this is an important distinction – actually want to be swept off your feet by Prince or Princess Charming – preferably with little or no effort on your part – and be carried away into the sunset?

If it's the latter put this book down. Return it to wherever you bought it from, and find another book. Walk away now. It's never gonna happen. It's not the *'carried away into the sunset'* bit that's impossible (although, that in itself is a tall order), it's the *'with little or no effort'*.

A rather bitter lady once told me, "life isn't a romantic comedy, Peter. The fairy tale just doesn't happen. Not in real life." Rather annoyingly, I think she may be right.

Now, odds are that you might be able to think of an example to prove me wrong.

"What," you might say, "about Dave and Sally? Jon and Gina? Gerald and Jim? Dertha and Gertha? They met at the bus stop, boarded the number 38, and several hours later (as the bus pulled into the depot) they were still chatting. And ever since that maiden voyage they've been blissfully happy. What about them?"

Well, firstly, I made all those couples up (apart from Jon and Gina – hey guys), but, secondly, I'll lay you money that the example you have in mind *isn't* quite the fairy tale you think it is. Chances are, that one of them, (perhaps both of them) were secretly (or not so secretly) on the look out for a partner. One or both of them were, in their own little way, doing whatever they could to increase the chances of meeting someone at the bus stop. Or the dry cleaners. Or the supermarket. Anywhere! That 'chance' encounter was anything but. The reality is, successful romances nearly always start with an investment of time, effort, often both.

I know of not one, but *two* ladies, who used to get up early in the morning to doll-themselves-up in order to walk the dog, and thereby accidentally-on-purpose bump into that cute guy with the Alsatian (not the same cute guy obviously – although thinking about it now, maybe it was. Hmmm). I have friends (Jon and Gina, again – hey guys) who after meeting at a conference travelled several stops further on the tube than they needed to, just so they could continue chatting to each other. And I know of one lady who, with a little diary shuffling, managed to organise three dates in a day. As well as do a full day's work at the office.

None of them are single now.

Let me introduce you to the inescapable laws of dating. Just like the laws of physics there's no way to avoid them – it's how things are. And here's the first.

DATING LAW #1:
DATING IS TOUGH. GET OVER IT.

Dating requires more than a little deliberation, perseverance, and determination. In many ways when you decide to 'start dating' you're setting out on a journey. One with masses of potential for disappointment, frustration, and disillusionment. Too many people give up, fall by the wayside and choose instead a life of bitter solitude. Others just keep stumbling down the same path, making the same mistakes over and over again, until they're so numb from the heartbreak and heartache that they wouldn't know love if it tapped them on the shoulder and handed them a business card. And still others 'settle for' – one of the saddest phrases in the English language – someone who becomes a constant reminder of what life could have been. Should have been.

It doesn't have to be that way.

If you're prepared to put the time in, play it smart, make some effort, dating can actually be lots and lots of fun. It's less of a journey – more of a ride. And you too can have that 'chance encounter on the bus'.

Ready?

Climb on board.

Let's get started.

Part 1

"So, how did you two meet?"

FINDING 'THE ONE'

Some authors have a lot to answer for. Fiction authors specifically. *Romantic* fiction authors, if we're really going to start pointing the finger.

At some point in the last hundred years or so, Prince Charming, the beautiful princess locked in the tower, and similar love-interests, made the transition from fairy tales, myth and legend, and became a part of mainstream culture. There's hardly a movie made today that doesn't have a romantic thread running through it, even if it's only a subplot. The age-old tale of 'boy meets girl' isn't a tale any longer. It's an expectation. It's how most of us expect our lives to play out, with only the slightest variation. We drift through life waiting for 'the one'.

Now, I'm not about to tell you that there's anything wrong with that (well, not quite yet anyway) – but I am going to suggest that you might be skipping a stage.

Here's something I'd like you to consider:

DATING LAW #2:
IN ORDER TO MEET
'THE ONE',
YOU MUST FIRST MEET
'THE MANY'

This part of the book is all about finding '*potential* partners'. We're going to call them 'potentials' for short, and the thing about 'potentials' is that they are just that; they're people who *might* be 'the one', but we won't know until we've grilled them over dinner, shared a nice bottle of wine or two, spent an afternoon walking along the Thames, seen a movie together, and finally figured out what they like for breakfast. Then we might know. Until then, they're a 'potential'.

And 'potentials' are good. And you should seek out as many as you can until you've found what you're looking for.

A few words on how this book works: most self help books invite you to dip in and out of the book as you see fit. This isn't one of those books. Whilst I'm not going to throw a hissy fit if you start skipping sections (I mean, how would I know?) I have tried to arrange the chapters in some sort of logical order such that if you work through the book, *completing the steps as you go*, the odds of you meeting potential partners – and therefore 'the one' you're looking for – will grow steadily.

So, for instance, in a chapter or two we'll, at the very least, take a look at online dating because, statistically, that's far more likely to work for you than anything else. After that we'll move on to social media and other 'online' ways of hunting down a potential. And finally, if you make it that far, we'll consider the pros and cons of Speed Dating events.

Now, if whilst we're doing all this a 'potential' turns up on the scene, and suddenly that turns into an actual date, bookmark wherever you are, and jump forward to *Part 2* (the chapter entitled 'Dates') where we'll discuss what to do next.

If the date doesn't pan out you can (and should) come right back and continue *Part 1* from where you left off. Remember dating law number 2; you can't meet 'the one' until you've met 'the many', and I'm afraid to say one 'failed' date doesn't constitute 'many'.

So, with all that in mind let's start by tracking down a few 'potentials'.

What Do You Want?

It's a funny thing about losing someone you care about. Every argument, every cross word, every lie, they all come back to haunt you. In your darkest moments, all you can think about is how you could have, should have, done things better.

But I've learnt a thing or two about pain in recent years, and one of those things is that it can be the start of something amazing. If you let it.

For me, it was the start of a quest for a better life – for happiness – a journey that I fully expect to last the rest of my life. But that's okay. Because sometimes the journey *is* the destination. Just ask anyone who loves to travel.

That said, I'm not a fan of wandering aimlessly. I like to know where I'm heading.

If you've read my first book, *How To Do Everything and Be Happy*, then you'll know how important it is, when embarking on a quest, to figure out just what it is you really want.

Most people I encounter haven't actually got a clue what they want. They might wake up in the morning and *want* to go back to bed. They might flick through a magazine and *want* those shoes. They might even *want* the person, in the magazine, wearing those shoes. But these desires come and go. Few of them seem to stick around and become important – which is odd because when you're growing up, figuring out *what you want* is very important and actively encouraged.

"What do you want for Christmas?"

"What do you want to do today?"

"What do you want to be when you grow up?"

A huge part of being a kid is spent working out what we want, and then writing it down or telling someone about it. And yet, as we get older, and we're finally in a position to do something about the bigger 'wants' of our childhood, we seem to give the question less and less thought. As if the day-to-day grind of making ends meet is more than enough to occupy every waking minute.

And that's a mistake.

Knowing exactly what you want is hugely important. Merely *knowing* has the power to change *everything*. And this is especially true when it comes to dating.

You might think – as I used to – that you have a particular 'type', and that your type can be defined with a simple set of parameters.

Maybe something like this:

- Blond
- Early thirties
- Nice smile
- Brown eyes
- GSOH (Good Sense of Humour)
- Average build
- Pert bum
- Nice figure
- Works with books
- Enjoys sex

I'm here to tell you that's absolute nonsense.

Whilst *some* of those things may affect how you feel about someone *initially*, most of them won't mean a thing within thirty minutes to a couple of days of your first meeting.

Does the colour of their hair or eyes really make that much of a difference to you? Surely what's more important is how you melt when they give you that 'look'. Do you really want a blond, or are you more interested in what happens when you run your fingers through their hair? Is the pertness of their posterior really such a deal breaker? Surely what's more important is that they ignite your passion, not how they go about it.

A better check-list might look like this:

- Someone who fills my day with sunshine
- Young at heart

- Always smiling
- Makes lots of eye contact
- Laughs at my jokes
- And makes me laugh
- Turns me on
- Really turns me on.
- No, I mean; really, REALLY turns me on.
- Has a passion for literature and stories
- Loves to get intimate

I'll wager that many of you are thinking, "yes, yes, yes! That's what I want! Gimme some of that!" Well, of course you are. And that's because, in scientific terms, you're no longer using the 'left' side of your brain to process a bunch of pointless facts, you're now using the 'right' side of your brain to imagine feelings.

I'd like you to take a moment to consider what it is, and who it is, you're looking for.

Let's start with 'the what'.

What sort of relationship are you looking for? A romance? Friendship? Marriage? An affair? A one-night-stand?

Are you expecting lots of passion? Excitement? Adventure? Something more relaxed? Comfortable? Routine? A mixture?

Will this 'relationship' be full-time? Part-time? Every now and then? Temporary?

The easiest way to bottom this out is to think about the sorts of things you'll get up to with your ideal person. Will you meet up in swanky hotel rooms for illicit encounters? Or are you hoping for quiet nights in front of the telly sharing a tub of exotic ice-cream?

Now let's think about 'the who'. What sort of person are you looking for? Loud and vivacious? Quiet and homely? A bit of both? If it helps, imagine what they look like – but try if you can to move past the size of their bust, the broadness of their chest, or the pertness of their behind – instead get to the core of who they are. Are they nerdy? Nice? Naughty? Sporty? Sassy? Sensual? Kind? Caring? Quirky?

What I want you to do is to create a very clear picture in your mind of the sort of relationship you see yourself in, and the sort of person you'll be sharing it with. And though you might not realise it yet, this really is incredibly important.

The Power Of Focus

Brains are amazing. Especially yours. Even mine has its moments. And one of the most fascinating mechanisms of the human brain is how it deals with 'focus'.

Have you ever noticed how when you buy a new car, or even when you've merely decided what type of car it is you want to buy, you start seeing that same car everywhere?

Or how you can see someone across a crowded room, start to walk towards them, and somehow collide with a pillar, a person, something else, that was directly in front of you but momentarily invisible?

That's the power of focus. It happens because in order for our brains to cope with the extraordinary amount of information coming in through our five senses from the world around us, we're programmed to concentrate on what's 'important' and pretty much ignore the rest. And who decides what's important to your brain?

You do.

The very act of figuring out what you're looking for in a potential date, and a subsequent relationship, will enable you to do two things:

Firstly, it'll make life significantly easier should you decide to use social media or one of the numerous online dating websites or apps. Do this work now and I pretty much guarantee that your profile will be substantially more interesting to read than the vast majority of your competitors.

Secondly, though, and perhaps more interestingly, it'll reprogram your subconscious to be on the look out for the very person you imagine. There's a very real chance that if you do this task correctly you'll meet the person of your dreams in real life. *You might not even need the rest of this book* – now how's that for getting your money's worth!

I first put myself through this exercise many years ago when I'd finally had enough of being single.

Until then, my attitude to dating, I'm ashamed to say, had been to pursue anybody who gave me a second glance. It wasn't that I didn't know what I wanted, it's just that I didn't think I could afford to be picky! There weren't that many single girls around – if I started drawing up a list of 'wants' I was worried that I'd reduce my already limited options to zero.

Then I came across the power of focus in a book about time management and wondered if it could be applied to life in general. After months, possibly even years, of less-than-satisfactory relationships with long periods of nothing in-between, I sat down and wrote out what I actually wanted. It was like writing a shopping list of qualities that I hoped for in my ideal person.

And about six weeks later I met Kate. My future wife.

Now – that's not the whole story, obviously. There were a few stages between writing my 'perfect woman shopping list' and choosing to sit next to this beautiful blonde I spied from across the room, but a few months into our relationship I looked back at that list and I was amazed at just how many of the criteria Kate met. Coincidence? Perhaps. But for the time it would take you to create your own list, isn't it worth the effort?

A word of warning: Concentrate on what you *want*, not what you don't want.

If you've just got out of a relationship you probably have a whole raft of qualities you want to *avoid* in your next partner, but the brain doesn't cope well with negatives. Trying *not* to think about something is actually impossible. The moment you decide *not* to think about your ex – boom! – there they are in the middle of your head, and the focus mechanism of your brain is now on the lookout for someone just like them.

If it helps, take all those negative qualities and turn them on their head. Was your ex particularly selfish? Then add 'thoughtful' to your shopping list. Was their idea of a great night out to go get a battered sausage from the local chippy? Add 'we go to fancy restaurants' to your wish list.

Action Points

Throughout this book there are various Action Points. These boxes serve as stop signs. The idea is that you stop, address the action, and then continue.

Now clearly, if you ignore the Action Point – the stop sign – it's unlikely that you'll be hit by a truck a moment later. Also, I'm not going to pursue you through the following pages, flag you down and issue you with a ticket and 3 points on your Amazon account. That's not going to happen.

Also, I've always been quite enthusiastic about 'ideas'. But whilst I like to collect and share ideas, I fully accept that you have just as much right to ignore them completely. I promise not to get annoyed with you for dismissing any suggestion (and these are only 'suggestions') I throw in your direction, if you promise to forgive me for being a little passionate, or teacher-ish.

That said, I'm assuming you bought this book because something in your head said "Hey – I want to master this dating thing…" and way back on page three, four, something like that, we agreed (well, you read it and I didn't hear you object) that you couldn't achieve this aim without putting a little effort in. So as I'm writing the words, addressing the Action Points is your part of the deal.

With all that in mind here's the first Action Point of the book, and it's a biggy!

STOP! ACTION POINT!

What do you want?

Put this book down, and spend just three or four minutes *writing down* exactly what and who you're looking for.

Use a computer if you can, and save the document somewhere you'll find it again. We'll be referring back to this document later.

Try and get beyond the facts and figures – what they look like and the things you'll have in common – move on to how the two of you will be together, what you'll get up to, and how that will feel. Describe, if you can, the perfect afternoon, an average day, your dream vacation, with this person in your life.

Above all, concentrate on what you want, not what you don't want.

GOING 'ONLINE'

Twenty five years ago, maybe longer, I worked in an office where people dictated letters and memos, and handed them to a secretary to type up. Our department was considered high tech; as well as a secretary, the five of us *shared* a PC. It wasn't networked. The internet didn't exist. I honestly have no idea how we got anything done.

Now the entire world is 'online'. My ten-year-old niece and nephew send me poems they've written, pictures they've taken or songs that they've made, electronically, from a variety of devices scattered around their house. They visit 'virtual worlds' where they create and take on the persona of 'monsters' and meet other children of the new millennium. And only occasionally does this hi-tech world fall short of their expectations. Like when my nephew recently expressed some frustration when he couldn't connect to Nana's WiFi.

"Nana doesn't have WiFi," said his dad.

"No WiFi!" replied my wide eyed nephew.

Welcome to the 21st Century.

Everyone's online.

Come and join in.

Step Away From The Mouse…

Whoa there! When I suggested you march confidently into that online world I didn't mean right this second!

This book is as much about *not* doing things, as doing things, and one of the things you definitely shouldn't be doing is signing up to the first dating site that takes your fancy[1]. Least not yet.

I am not known for my patience. In fact, I think it's fair to say that I am the most impatient person I know. Patience is for people who have time. I don't have nearly enough. Being patient takes too long.

That said, a lifetime of screwing stuff up and having to sort it out later, merely because I rushed whatever I was doing in the first place, has taught me that good preparation is *everything*.

This is particularly true of online dating, and whereas you might be keen to sign-up and get started, a little planning now will save *months* of heartache later on. So bear with me for a chapter or three whilst we make sure you have everything in place.

Let's start with the most important element first.

---

[1] If you're already signed up to a dating website, or *Tinder*, or you frequent social media, don't panic, maybe just read a bit faster.

PHOTOS

All online dating and social media websites and apps not only allow you to upload a selection of photos, some even *insist* upon it. And without a doubt your photo, or photos, are THE most important part of your online persona – at least they are if you want to use the web to find a potential. Without photos you're pretty much wasting your time.

As getting your photos right is so important, it might take us (and by us, I mean you!) a few days to find and decide on the best selection of images, so it's probably best we get started right away.

Now, it could be you're one of those folks who believe that "looks aren't important", and if you are it might be tempting to skip this stage altogether. But ironically whilst you've reached a level of enlightenment that transcends the superficial, you are – I'm afraid to say – in the minority.

Take for instance my pals Jon and Rachel[2]. I met them at a dinner party, and at the time they were coming up to their second wedding anniversary, so I asked them how they met. Actually, what I really asked was "did you meet online?" to which they said "yes." They joined e-harmony, and within a week they'd arranged to meet, got totally smitten with each other, and terminated their memberships. Pretty amazing, eh? Even more so when I tell you that Rachel was one of the 'photo-less profile' brigade. I raised an eyebrow, but Jon assured me that (and I quote), "looks aren't important." Quite how he managed to say this without getting a thump in the arm I have no idea.

But here's the thing – *it was Rachel who contacted Jon*. And whilst her lack of a photo didn't put Jon off, Jon's photo *was* what drew her to his profile. There he was, a strapping figure of manliness, glowing from his experience of having completed the Three Peaks Challenge,

---

[2] This is a different Jon to the one married to Gina. I know. It's confusing.

and the first thought that went through her mind was, something along the lines of, "what a rugged hero of a bloke."

Photos *are* important. Whether you decide to sign-up to *Tinder*, a traditional, dating website, or just to continue messing around on *Twitter* or *Facebook*, the first thing that people – and by that we mean *potentials* – will look at, are your photos. In fact, your *lead*-photo (the one that you decide is the best of the bunch) will probably be the very reason someone decides to look at your profile at all. It's the virtual equivalent of someone spotting you from across a crowded room and deciding to wander over to – maybe not to introduce themselves – but certainly to take a closer look.

Here's the bad news though, one *bad* photo can neutralise half a dozen good ones and render anything else on your profile utterly useless. So, let's begin by discussing what you're *not* going to do.

No No No And Again No...

There are a few pictures that should never, ever be on your dating profile, or used as your primary picture on social media. Let's kill those off now.

Big No No #1: Using pictures of someone else

Selecting photos is a pain. It's not enjoyable. It feels like work. It takes far too long. You can't help thinking that the path to romance just shouldn't be this difficult.

Faced with this heinous task you wouldn't be the first person in the world to wonder if there are *short-cuts*. For instance, wouldn't it just be quicker to find a pic of *someone else* – maybe someone who looks a bit like you? Not necessarily a celebrity, maybe just some Joe, or Joanna, someone with whom you have a few physical traits in common. It wouldn't be lying exactly – you could even put something in the profile explaining that whilst this isn't a pic of you, you're not that dissimilar and you can send a real pic on request. What's wrong with that?

It won't work.

At least not on your average online dating website.

An interesting thing has happened in recent years. As dating sites have increased in popularity they've become prime hunting ground for fraudsters, and con-artists. Whilst the majority of the people you'll encounter on these sites are hoping to steal your heart, a few are hoping to steal your bank balance. These nefarious individuals are understandably reluctant to use images of themselves so they merely do as you're considering, and use an image of someone else. We'll talk more about how to spot and avoid these people later in the book, but for now you need to realise that as a consequence, dating sites, and the people who use them, have become hyper-sensitive to fake-photos.

Not only will your photos usually undergo some sort of check (by a human) before they're visible on your profile, but most sites have a mechanism that enables other members to 'flag' anything suspicious. You only need one savvy member (such as myself) to flag your fake pic and moments later it – and possibly your entire profile – could be removed.

And here's something you might not know; it's surprisingly quick and simple to check to see whether an image appears elsewhere on the internet. We'll be using this technique to our own advantage in a few chapters time, but for now you can assume that any image you put on a dating website is going to be checked and double checked numerous times.

Of course, on social media, people are far more laid back about photos. It's social media! Its purpose is to fill those long, long hours when you should be working. It's not supposed to be used as a dating tool. No one's going to object if your primary picture is of someone else, your favourite cartoon character, a photo of smiley face drawn in the froth of a cappuccino, or that really great one of you back in the day.

Or are they?

Big No No #2: Using old pictures (when you had hair / were thin / etc)

The pictures you pick should represent how you look *right now*.

It's human nature to wish we looked a bit more like we did in our late teens and early twenties, back when we could button our jeans and the most challenging thing about our hairline was trying to find something to secure those flowing locks in place. But that was then, and this is now. And whilst you obviously want your pictures to be as flattering as possible, when you eventually get to go on that first date you want the other person to think you look ever so slightly *better* in the flesh. Don't fall into that trap of thinking that you'll have established so much rapport beforehand that they'll somehow fail to notice that you're at least ten years older than you are in your photos. They won't. They'll feel conned. And even if they don't say something right away it's likely to gnaw away at their soul, and ultimately kill the relationship.

How do I know all this?

Because it's happened to me.

Twice.

Many, many years ago I arranged a date with a cute, petite, brunette, and consequently failed to recognise the much larger, slightly greying lady who walked through the door of the pub. And then there was the time I almost sat myself at the table of a stunning blonde, when I suddenly realised that the blonde standing at the till – considerably less stunning and currently buying the world's largest cream cake – had the foreign accent I'd been expecting of my date.

Both times, I sat on the other side of the table feeling slightly duped, whilst at the same time wondering whether I should say something – but what can you say? My irritation subsided slightly when both ladies turned out to be charming and fun – but I was left with this underlying sense of sadness. Like we'd had a row that we were now trying to put behind us. My mind kept going back to the photos – and how this girl opposite me wasn't her! She was her older, less attractive, big sister. Here I was, ten minutes into a new relationship and already I wanted someone else.

I never saw either lady again after those first dates.

I know what you're thinking. You're thinking, "Jonsey, you're so shallow." And maybe you're right. But I'm not the only one. A friend once told me how she went for a date with a gentleman who turned out to be *twenty years* older than the picture on his dating profile. She sat there all evening, fuming, and composing an email rant in her head that she would send him when she got home[3]. I'm not sure who I feel more sorry for.

In stark contrast, however, there have been two occasions where ladies I've arranged to meet, who were pretty darn attractive in their photos to start with, turned out to be drop dead gorgeous in real life! Now that's the way to start a date!

---

[3] How terribly British.

Big No No #3: Close-up face-only pictures

A popular trick amongst the more body-conscious folks, is to crop all their pictures so close that they're only showing their face.

Don't do this.

Make sure that amongst your photos there's at least one, preferably more, that are full or three quarter length.

Unless you're planning to sneak up behind your date and spent the entire evening with your face mere inches from theirs, it's going to be virtually impossible to prevent them from seeing your figure. And whilst you're probably hoping that your charming personality will be more than enough to make up for those *extra* curves you'd prefer not to have, you might not get that opportunity: I know of one lady whose date spied her from across the street, turned round, and promptly legged it in the opposite direction! Now, clearly, he was a horrible person, and she'd been spared an evening with someone who didn't deserve to know how lovely she was – but she didn't see it like that at the time. She felt wretched, and what little confidence she had was ground into dust.

Spare yourself that pain. It's better to be upfront and honest about the figure you have or haven't got. They're going to find out sooner or later; it might as well be now.

And guys, don't start assuming that this doesn't somehow apply to us. It does. There's a school of thought that says that women aren't as concerned about physical appearance as us chaps, but I simply don't believe it. They take in *everything*! From whether you're wearing the 'wrong' shoes to whether your jacket fits properly. In many ways this advice is even more important for men.

Big No No #4: Close-up body part pictures

Let's talk about *other* popular close-ups.

There are ladies who think they're being cute and mysterious with a picture of a beautifully framed eye, complete with long luscious lashes. And there are guys who are firmly convinced they're making every hot-blooded woman weak at the knees with a close up of their genitalia.

The reality is, most people find the eyeball-ladies and the penis-guys a little dull, and the tiniest bit annoying.

Now, a creative shot of your shirt falling off your shoulder, clearly showing your anchor tattoo, and cropped so we can just see your cheeky smile – that might work, so long as it's mixed in with some full length shots. Or one of your legs, lying on the couch, bound in rope, with a kitchen timer off to one side – that's intriguing, so long as it's not the only pic you have. Regardless of whether you're a guy or a gal, both these images would be quite interesting, and when combined with a selection of proper pictures they'd let the rest of the world know that there's far more to you than just an eyeball. Or a penis.

There's no getting away from the fact that unless you're looking for some sort of internet/email-only relationship there's little point in trying to hide what you look like. Sooner or later someone's going to meet you and when that happens you want it to be a pleasant surprise, rather than a nasty shock. The companion guide to this book[4] has an entire section dedicated to improving and making the most of your appearance but *right now* we need to work with what you've got. And that might not be as difficult as you think.

For instance, there's one body of research[5] that suggests that ladies who are generally considered 'attractive' receive *less* messages than those who divide opinion and might be considered stunning by some, and less so by others. Being a lady of distinctive looks – such as someone who is very curvy, has a mass of freckles, long flowing ginger locks, or an arm full of tattoos – is *scientifically proven* to work in your favour… *if* you play to your strengths.

Now that's the kind of science I like!

---

[4] '*How To Be Even More Attractive*' – available from amazon or wherever you got this book.
[5] Links to all the original research referenced by this book are on the website.

Big No No #5: Photos of you with other people

Back in 2014, when the first edition of this book came out, there were only 4 big no-nos. This section, and the one that follows, didn't exist.

But then *Tinder* came along.

Because *Tinder* uses photos taken from your *Facebook* profile it's now all too easy to build a dating profile made up entirely of photos of you and your mates on one of your many drunken nights out.

But is that a bad thing? I mean, there you are, all glammed up, clearly having the time of your life. That's bound to attract someone of a similar party-like demeanor surely?

Stop! Just… stop.

Firstly, those same scientists from the last section *also* discovered that photos where people are drinking do statistically worse than pictures where people *aren't* drinking. Who knew! If you have pictures of yourself with a glass of *Prosecco* in your hand, or a bottle of beer, ditch 'em. Those photos do not belong on your profile.

More importantly than that though, the last thing you want to do is make someone have to figure out which of the drunken people in the photograph is actually you – *particularly* if, and let's be brutally honest here, other people in the photo *might* be considered marginally more attractive than your good self.

Even if you're 100% certain that you're the hotty amongst your chosen group of pals, why take the chance? Attractiveness just isn't that simple. Your so-called less attractive friend – the curvy one with the ginger hair, freckles, and an arm full of tattoos – might actually trump you in some circles. Science says so.

This group-photo advice goes double for pictures of you with someone of the opposite sex[6]. Ninety per cent of people will assume that the person with their arms draped around you is your ex – the other ten per cent will suspect that it's your *current* partner. *No one* will ever believe it's your brother or sister – not even if you tell them otherwise!

---

[6] Or same sex, if you're gay.

How can you fix this? Well you could fire up *Photoshop* and try to obscure the faces of anyone who isn't you, or you could try and crop the photo so tight that only the odd ear or hand of your 'sister' is left in the shot. But it won't work. The damage is done.

Almost as bad as the group-photo, or the photo of you with your 'not-my-girlfriend/boyfriend-honest', is the photo of you with kids, be they yours or anyone else's. Maybe you want your prospective partner to know you're good with kids, or you want to underline the fact that you come as part of a package? I can understand that, but those sort of details belong in your self summary (which we'll come to in a couple of chapters), not here in your photos.

The only person in your profile photos should be *you*.

Period.

Big No No #6: Duck face

So, you've decided against passing off pictures of Rita Ora as yourself. You've reluctantly ditched those fantastic pictures of you taken over a decade ago. And the ones of you and your pals on your last drunken excursion – despite the fact you looked fabulous – have been deleted. What you have left are a selection of reasonably current full-length photos. And there you are, pouting provocatively for the camera.

Except you're not.

It's a rare person that can pull off 'the pout', and let me be the first to point out that you're *not* that person. Right now you look more like Daffy Duck! So stop that! Just look into the camera, think about something that makes your insides go gooey, and smile godammit!

Unless you're a man.

Let's take a look at some scientifically proven tips on what photos to pick, and how to make yourself instantly more photogenic.

Yes Yes Yes!

So, what sort of photos should you pick? Well, that's a good question, and fortunately one that's been the subject of quite a lot of research. Grab your digital camera, and prepare to smile. Or not.

To smile, or not-to-smile?

For many, many years I've had a strong interest in photography, and to make a few quid on the side I've taken portfolio and publicity photographs for friends or colleagues. Some of the ladies I've photographed have gone on to be glamour models – and of those that did, the ones that were the most successful, were the ones with the biggest…

Smile.

This makes me feel a whole lot better about us men and is backed up by research that says for maximum man-appeal[7], girls should smile into the camera, and for a little extra oomph, make a flirty, playful or "come and get me" face.

The same research, however, says that us guys should do the *exact opposite*. We should look moodily off into the distance, as though we're pondering the next line of a sonnet.

None of the research explains why this should be the case – all we have are the numbers. When the analysts drew up their charts and graphs, *on average* the moody guys and the smiley girls did a lot better than the smiley guys and the moody girls – at least in terms of the number of messages they got.

Now, this doesn't mean that you're doomed should you happen to be a girl with a bunch of moody pictures to pick from, or if (like me) you're a guy who can't help grinning like a maniac into the camera, but if you can, pick at least a couple of photos following the advice above.

---

[7] Or presumably girl-appeal if you're lesbian – though the research doesn't say.

Interestingly, making a flirty face *away* from the camera (at someone or something else other than the photographer) is bad bad *bad* for both sexes. Intriguing isn't it! If you have photos like that, discard them now.

From above or below?

Most people are familiar with the classic *'Myspace'* photo, where the subject of the photograph has taken a self portrait by holding their camera phone at arm's length, slightly above their head, and looking up. What these people possibly didn't realise, but what photographers have known for years, is that this is a significantly more flattering angle than simply taking a photo straight on, or worse, from below.

I know what you're thinking, but it has nothing to do with cleavage. This angle works just as well for guys and for ladies who cover up. It's just a better angle, and consequently the numbers show that it dramatically increases your chances of getting contacted.

If you haven't got a *'Myspace'* style photo, why not grab your camera or phone, step into a well lit room and take one now?

To cover up – or not?

If you're fella, and blessed with nice abs, then despite numerous pieces of advice to the contrary, taking your shirt off turns out to be the *second* most effective thing you can do to boost your attractiveness in your photos. This is rather gutting to those of us whose shirtless days are either long-gone or never arrived.

Likewise, the research we have also proves that showing a degree of cleavage significantly increases the number of contacts you'll get. Now there's a shock.

What's more interesting, however, is that the cleavage shot is actually more powerful the *older* you get, and allows the older lady to level the playing field with her younger rivals, and to completely leave behind ladies of a similar age who have chosen to cover up.

Of course, whilst displaying a little flesh increases the amount of attention you *get*, it might not necessarily be the attention that you *want.* To get anything more interesting than single worded messages from all and sundry you'll need something more in your photos than a nice chest.

The Activity Shot

Smiling (or not), unbuttoning your top, or holding the camera above your head are all great strategies – but they're nowhere near as powerful as *'the activity shot'*. If you're photographed *doing something* then not only will it get you a better quality of message, but potentially it'll get you more of them!

Why would that be? Well, chiefly it gives the person viewing your photos something to comment on, but from a photographer's point of view, I suspect that pictures like this feel less posed, and more genuine. There's a sense that we're seeing the real person.

From this perspective, when selecting your profile pictures, those pictures of you taken by friends (and tagged on *Facebook*) are probably a better place to start than the makeover shoot you went on last year.

You might be wondering if the type of activity makes a difference. It does.

Being photographed with an animal appears to be the most powerful of all the potential activity photos. If you have photos of you petting your dog or feeding a horse, upload them to your profile.

Photos of you playing an instrument exude extreme coolness and give any potential a very obvious conversation starter.

Strangely though, outdoor photos, and 'travel photos' don't seem to do well (statistically speaking).

Natural light

Finally, before we knuckle down and select some photos for your profile, let's talk about lighting. All the research backs up what portrait photographers have known for years that flash photography or harsh lighting make you look older. Try – if you can – to pick photos that were taken in good natural light.

Enough already – time for some action!

Pick A Selection Of Photos!

Right. Here's what I suggest you do:

Sit down at your computer, and gather together all the photos you have of yourself, whether they be on your hard-drive or online (such as *Facebook*). *Copy* them to a folder (leave the original where it is), then once you're sure you have them all, trawl through them several times doing the following:

On the first pass, delete any photos taken over two years ago, or where you're pictured with (more attractive) friends, or where the lighting is harsh.

On the second, pick out the pictures where you're smiling into the camera (if you're a girl) or looking moodily into the distance (if you're a guy). Pick out any interesting action shots, photos of you with animals, playing an instrument etc. Pick any pictures where the camera was above you, and – if you're brave enough – any cleavage or ab shots.

On the third pass, go through this final selection and pick between six and nine of the very best, avoiding if you can, pictures that are very similar to each other, or obviously taken at the same event.

Finally, go through this selection and pick just one photo to use as your lead picture. By all means pick your favourite, but make sure it'll work well when it's reduced to the size of a thumbnail.

Now, if you've done all that without breaking down in tears or wanting to toss this book across the room, I congratulate you. I'm also slightly envious. If on the other hand you're more like me then I'm guessing after the second pass, maybe even the first, you were probably left with only one photo (that you might not even like), or no photos at all.

It's at this point that you need to do one of two things, perhaps even both.

Firstly, find a trusted friend, get them to read this chapter, and then go through the above exercise again allowing them the last word on whether a photo makes it into your final selection.

Secondly, if the two of you *really* can't find any photos, you need to take some! In all honesty, this is sometimes the easiest solution. Get a couple of bottles of wine, invite your trusted friend over one well-lit afternoon (tell them to bring their dog/horse), and wearing as many different outfits as you can, using every room in the house, host your own dating profile photo-shoot. Take as many different pictures as possible, from interesting angles (but never below). Remember to change your facial expression. Put on some loud music if it helps. Dance around. Have fun.

STOP! ACTION POINT!

Select your profile photos

- Don't 'hide'. You want people to be pleasantly surprised when they eventually meet you, not disappointed.
- Don't use group shot photos.
- Don't do the 'duck face'.
- Keep in mind all the things that are statistically proven to work:

a) The 'activity' shot is most powerful of all.

b) The 'Myspace' angle is more flattering.

c) Showing a great set of abs actually works.

d) A hint of cleavage allows you to compete with the younger woman.

e) Avoid using 'flash' – pick photos taken in strong natural light.

f) If you polarize opinions on attractiveness, play to those strengths.

- If you're struggling, get a trusted friend to help you choose the final selection, or take some new photos.
- Decide which photo will be your lead.
- Finally, <u>don't</u> sign up to *Tinder* or an online dating account just yet – we've still got work to do.

Potential Photo Problems

Right then. Who's still struggling with their photos? There seem to be a handful of common reasons that prevent people from putting photos on their profiles. Let's see if we can deal with them here.

I don't have photos on my computer

Time and time again, I see dating profiles from people claiming they don't have any pictures on their computer.

If you only have photos printed on photographic paper (how quaint), and you don't have the ability to scan them in (how old are these pictures anyway?) try thinking outside the box a little:

Are there pictures on *another* computer? You wouldn't be the first person to tell me you haven't got any photos on your computer, when there's an entire folder on your *home/work* computer, your laptop, or your phone.

No joy? Okay. Have you been anywhere recently where someone may have taken your picture? A party or other social event? Can you contact someone and see if they can email you something?

Still photo-less? Hmmm. Are you on *Facebook*? No? This might just be a good enough reason to sign-up. Unless you're a complete recluse I'll bet my next royalty cheque that there are *already* images of you, taken by someone you know, on the *Facebook* servers. Why not join up and browse the photo libraries of your friends and colleagues.

There are no photos of me in existence, anywhere

Seriously? Well then, time to get a friend over and take some.

I have no friends (with a digital camera)

Then I'm afraid it's time to bite the bullet and take some photos yourself (why not try *the Myspace angle* described a few pages back). And before you tell me that you have no camera, or phone with a camera built in, now might be the time to invest in one. There's no need to break the bank, digital cameras – especially second hand ones – are surprisingly cheap (you can find plenty, on Amazon, around the twenty pound mark). Stick to a well known make and you won't go far wrong.

I'm a complete technophobe!

A friend pointed out that for many, the problem wouldn't be a lack of suitable photos – most of us own smart phones and laptops and desktops all stuffed full of digital images – the challenge would be getting those images out! Apparently, not everyone has my level of geekiness and knows how to navigate the contents of their computer's hard drive.

If you're technology challenged friends fear not – I have two solutions:

The first involves befriending a geek – *not me*, I hasten to add; I have more than my quota of friends for whom I'm their personal IT helpdesk. Someone else. Someone you trust. Someone patient. Someone who can sit down with you, and teach you how to find your photos, as well as how to copy them, or move them around.

The second is simply to type into *Google* "how do I find all the images on my…", insert name of computer or smart phone here, and browse the results you get back. You'll be stunned at the number of free step-by-step guides and webpages people have created to help folks like you. Some are better than others. Keep browsing until you find one you like the look of.

I'm overweight / old / ugly

There's a school of thought that online dating is only for the slender, the young and the very, very beautiful.

That is, of course, complete and utter tosh.

Yes, the young, the slender, and the very beautiful have always had an easier time at dating – online or otherwise – but those preconceived ideas you may have that you have to be any, or all, of those things, and that men/women are *only* looking for people of a certain age, or a body type, are – and I'm speaking from experience – nonsense.

I won't lie to you – online dating is a *lot* more difficult than the television or internet ads would have us believe. Finding a 'special someone' who's looking for a 'special someone just like you' will take some doing, but more damaging than your size, shape or age is your *belief* that those things matter.

They don't.

I realise, of course, how hard it can be to accept that fact when all the evidence appears to be to the contrary, but I know from my own experience that you're jumping to the wrong conclusions. Right now, get up off the coach, go over to the nearest mirror and take a look at your reflection. Go ahead. This'll only take a second.

See that person?

They're fabulous.

In their own special way, there's something about that person in the mirror that makes them attractive to a fair few people out there. Not just one – a *fair few.* You don't have to take my word for it – I'm going to prove it to you. And to do so I need you to find half a dozen photos.

I'm married / a famous celebrity / I want to stay anonymous

Finally, a legitimate reason for not wanting to upload your picture to the internet.

If it's important for you not to be recognised by friends, family, neighbours or co-workers then bear with me. There's an entire section, just for you, in a few pages time.

DATING WEBSITES & APPS

It's astonishing to think that online dating has really only been around for a few years. Although the internet has been with us a while, at the turn of the century there were only about half a dozen English-speaking dating sites worth bothering with. *Match.com* (arguably the first proper dating site) didn't launch officially until 1998.

By my calculations, online dating websites and apps are responsible for one in five marriages[8]. Include relationships that haven't got as far as the altar, throw in the likes of *Facebook* and other social media, and I estimate 50 per cent of all romances probably start on the internet. Which is pretty interesting. Fascinating, in fact. It means that, statistically, online dating is possibly your best option *even if* you choose to ignore everything I say from here on. But stick with me and I'll improve those odds further still.

Resistance is futile

Now, there will be those amongst you who may be experiencing some resistance to the idea of online dating. Maybe you've tried that already, or think you have. Maybe you've heard one too many horror stories. Maybe you're all *Tinder*-ed out. Maybe you're on a budget. Maybe you're a technophobe. Maybe you don't want the stigma of being associated with 'the great unloved'… whatever your reason, bear with me a little longer. There are gems to be had in the pages that follow. And even if they're not enough to convince you to try out online dating, many of the tips, tricks and techniques I'm going to discuss work just as well on *other* online 'platforms'. To save me

---

[8] Check my numbers at *HowToStopWaitingAndStartDating.com*

repeating myself I will refer back to them, so don't toss me in the recycling just yet.

Instead, let's take a look at exactly what these dating websites do, how do they work, and what's going on behind that glossy exterior full of promises and pictures of laughing couples.

Traditional Dating Websites / Apps

Whilst dating sites and apps might use different techniques to try and entice you in – maybe the option to browse a few members, or perform a basic search for people in your area, or read a few testimonials – once you're through the marketing hype the vast majority function in exactly the same way.

After giving the site your email address, you're nearly always asked to specify whether you're male or female, how old you are, where in the world you live, and the sex of your preferred date.

Most sites will also ask how tall you are, your hair colour, your skin colour, and your build. Some sites might ask whether you're married, divorced, widowed, 'seeing someone' or 'available'. Whether you went to university? How much do you earn? Have you any kids? Do you want any? Still others might ask how often you drink alcohol, whether you're a vegan, vegetarian or meat eater, whether you smoke, and if so, what.

Should you answer all of these questions? And if so how truthful should you be? We'll find out a little later.

Once you've completed the 'Basic Information' most sites will ask you to write a 'Self Summary'; a paragraph or two where you're expected to sum yourself up for potential suitors. Some sites might break this into headings ('about me', 'what I'm looking for right now', 'six things I can't live without' etc). At least one site I know of has an ingenious point and click function where you can construct your profile from sentences that have already been written for you.

Pretty much every dating website and app also actively encourages you to upload as many pictures as you can. These pictures, the self-summary, and the basic information, make up your 'profile'.

Once you've created your 'profile' you can begin browsing others. Find one you like the look of and usually you can send the owner a message via the site's message system. Just as you would on *Facebook* or other social media websites.

Most of the websites offer various other 'functions' too: You can add people to a list of 'favourites'. You can send them a 'wink', a 'wave', or countless other virtual gestures. If you stumble across someone particularly repellent you can usually 'hide' them, so you never see them again, or 'block' them, so you never receive any of their winks, waves or messages. If you really dislike someone, or something, you can 'flag' it to the powers that be, whereby a crack team of operatives supposedly look into your complaint. As you might expect, this works better on some sites than others.

Some websites have 'chatrooms', or 'forums'. Others allow you to blog, or write a journal. Some have quizzes, or tests. A whole world of virtual wonders await you.

To a lesser degree dating apps offer pretty much the same experience.

Either way, all this virtual activity takes place online. In many ways it can feel like you've entered a virtual party where the wine keeps flowing and the music never stops. And just like its real-world counterparts, this party can feel lonely and bewildering.

Well fear not, brave warrior. Because you are not alone. Together, we're going to march confidently into that online world, and take it by storm.

Finding A Website (Or App) That's Right For You

So – which site (or app) should you pick? Maybe the most popular? Everyone seems to be using *Tinder* at the moment. Or maybe the biggest? That would seem logical, wouldn't it? Maximise your chances of finding Mr/Miss/Mrs Right (or Right Now)? Or maybe a free site? If it doesn't work out then all you've invested is time. Or what about that site you saw advertised on TV – you know, the one where the cute guy starts singing to the shy girl on a railway platform, and then they accidently tie their shoe laces together, and after filling out a simple ten minute love-match questionnaire, they stand together on that bridge and she asks him to marry her, and after he's thought about it for a bit he turns and says, "tomorrow?"

Let's take a look at some of your options:

Tinder

Just after the first edition of this book was published a new player entered the dating market place – one that stole a few clever ideas that had been done elsewhere, and then combined them into something we'd never seen before. Behold; *Tinder*.

Tinder is incredibly popular and it's easy to see why.

Firstly it is, for the main part, completely free. Whilst you can pay for some advanced features, you can browse, contact, and be contacted, by other *Tinder* users without limitation, and without shelling out a single penny.

Secondly, it's an app (and *only* an app) – and people like apps. It's designed to be used on your phone, though it will work on your iPad or other tablets.

Thirdly, it's easy to set up. Whilst you *can* create a *Tinder* profile with a valid mobile phone number, by far the easier (and in my opinion, safer) way is to link it to your *Facebook* account – so there's none of that thinking up a new password nonsense. You don't have to specify your age, or sex – it pulls all that information straight in.

You can write a profile if you like, but it's not obligatory, so most people don't bother. And when it comes to adding your photos, you just pick from the ones you've already got on FB. Easy.

Finally, it's really easy to use. You're presented with pictures of people within a given radius of your current location. If you like the look of them, swipe that picture up or to the right. If they're not blowing your skirt up, swipe them to the left. As soon as you *swipe right* (or up) on someone who's done the same to you, *Tinder* tells the both of you and a message box opens! It couldn't be more simple. It's almost… *fun!*

No more spending ages building a profile. No more figuring out whether this account is genuine or not. No more messages from people you don't want to hear from. The future of online dating has arrived!

Or has it?

No.

In my humble opinion, *Tinder* has made dating harder than ever. And nowadays, whenever I meet someone who's 'had it with online dating', it's nearly *always* because of *Tinder*. In an effort to make the online dating experience as easy as possible, *Tinder* has actually made it *harder*. Way to go *Tinder*.

Sure, you'll be presented with a seemingly endless supply of single people *right on your doorstep*. And because they all have to have a *Facebook* account you won't have to worry (so much) about scammers, spammers, or cam-girls. Neither will you have to worry about accidentally being matched with one of your *Facebook* pals – that's all taken care of. So you can actually afford to be really, *really* picky. And when you get a match – which you will – you'll probably assume (wrongly) that your single days are numbered.

They're not.

What awaits you is on the other side of the matching game (because a *game* is exactly what it is) is all the frustration and heartache that you thought you'd avoided by picking this app over the more traditional dating websites, and what you'll come to realise (or at least you should, if you stop to think about it for a moment) is that there's a darn sight more to successful online dating that merely sorting pretty pictures from the not-so-pretty.

Having said all that, whilst *Tinder* isn't the best online dating solution out there, it certainly isn't the worst. And actually, if you stop treating it like a 'game', put some work in, and adopt some nifty ninja-like dating strategies (which we'll cover as you work through this book) you *can* get it to work in your favour. I did. So keep that in mind as we continue.

Bumble

Hard though it might seem to believe, *Tinder* isn't the only dating app out there. Neither is it the only one that adopts a swipe right / left / up / down methodology. Let's have a quick look at *Bumble*.

Like *Tinder*, *Bumble* links to your *Facebook* profile. *Unlike Tinder*, *Bumble* isn't just for dating. Theoretically it can also be used for networking, or finding new friends – though a cynical person might claim this is just a built in excuse for when your spouse finds the app on your phone and asks why you've got it.

Also like *Tinder* it's free – ish – easy to use, and doesn't really care about all that profile text nonsense. In fact, on *Bumble* there's even *LESS* space to write something witty and charming. Yay! Who needs words anyway!? Everyone knows that in a hundred years we'll all be speaking emoji! Get with the times people.

And if you're really not a fan of words – and you're male – then rejoice! Because even if you match with someone, *Bumble* doesn't allow men to send the first message! It's up to *women* to make the first move. What's more they only have 24 hours to do so before you disappear off their radar forever.

Now all that might sound great if you're lazy, male, or hate sending messages, but it does also mean that your photos have to be *awesome*, your profile <u>sentence</u> has to be *awesome*, and the ladies you like the look of...? They need to be bold as brass.

Good luck with that.

Best move on quickly and treat *Bumble* with the contempt it deserves.

Membership Sites

Let's return to regular dating websites, whether they have an associated 'app' or not.

The majority of traditional dating websites usually require a membership fee of some description. Even a site that claims to be "free to join," *usually* only lets you browse member profiles, build your own, or answer a series of short questions. The moment you actually want to contact someone, you'll need to 'upgrade' to a 'premium' membership – which inevitably involves the use of a credit or debit card.

How much you can expect to pay varies dramatically. You could end up parting with anything from a few quid a month to well over thirty. Most sites offer substantial discounts if you sign up for three, six or even a twelve month membership... which is a little odd if you think about it. Shouldn't a really good dating site be able to match you with a suitable partner in a matter of weeks? Keep that thought at the back of your mind.

There is an argument that people who are prepared to put their hand in their pocket and pay for a dating service might be significantly more serious about finding a partner than, say, those who signed up, on a whim, to a free site. One imagines that there might also be considerably less fake profiles, scammers, and weirdoes. Maybe. But back in July 2013 the BBC investigative journalism television show 'Panorama' uncovered worrying evidence that far from stamping out fake profiles and scammers, *some* membership dating sites might actually be in the habit of creating their own fake profiles, and using them to seduce members into renewing their membership. There was even speculation as to whether communication between *genuine* members was being *suppressed* to reduce the possibility of newly formed couples leaving the site.

Now, according to the BBC's website, some of the claims in the programme have, or are currently, being disputed, but I can see how it could happen. A membership dating site's commercial success relies on *paying* members. But how do you get those members if you don't have any to begin with? And how do you persuade members to stay if they insist on pairing off and living happily ever after?

I have, of course, no idea whether this practice continues today, and for my own legal protection I'm not going to mention the company who Panorama accused of such unethical behaviour. What I *am* going to say is that having used several membership sites in the past, some are significantly better than others. If you really want to part with your money, pick a larger, better known dating website.

Onwards then.

'Specialist' Sites

Inevitably, as online dating becomes more popular – and presumably more profitable – new sites enter the market. And as it's difficult to compete with the likes of *Match.com* one way to do so is to *specialise*, and create a website appealing to a particular group of people – a 'niche' if you like.

There are dating sites for single parents, over forties, over fifties, Jewish folk, church goers, pretty much every skin colour on the planet, people whose line of work involves wearing a uniform, people who enjoy wearing a uniform for fun, sugar daddies, sugar mummies, toy boys, toy girls… and a huge number of sites whose primary focus is less about love and romance, and more about sex – whether that be a particular *type* of sex, or just someone willing to keep the sex hush hush. There are *even* sites for people who aren't looking for love, romance, or sex – but 'friendship'!

And though they're not really 'niche' I'd be remiss if I didn't mention the sites catering specifically to the gay and lesbian community.

It's worth mentioning that whilst a handful of these sites are free, most work on a membership basis. Many seem to be nothing more than money making ventures, as if there's a team of people somewhere thinking of new websites to create. "Pink Shoe Lovers – lets build a website for them!"

Beware of any site where it's, a) difficult/impossible to see how much they charge before you've signed up, b) where it's virtually impossible to tell who's a paid up member (and therefore someone who can reply to you without shelling out cash).

Free Sites

If, like Lennon & McCartney, you're of the opinion that "money can't buy me love", then you'll be pleased to know that there are a growing number of sites that don't require any sort of fee, and usually make their money from advertising.

Back in the early days, free sites were often littered with fake and joke profiles, scam artists, people selling either themselves or something else, and the downright strange. Imagine the trading floor of New York Stock Exchange – only with a few drunks, weirdoes and the odd prostitute thrown in for good measure. Now you have some idea of what belonging to one of the more popular free sites used to be like.

This was extremely frustrating – especially to the online dating newbie. Whereas you might think that a free site would be a good way to dip your toe in the online dating pond, the reverse used to be true.

But times have moved on. The larger free sites are getting better and better at keeping the riff-raff out, and whilst they're by no means perfect, right now[9] I personally believe most are easily as good as, *if not better*, than the non-free alternatives.

If you're both a born romantic *and* an old cynic (much like myself), and you've mastered some of the lessons contained within the pages of the tome you hold within your hands, then why waste your money on a membership site? You'll be able to walk amongst that trading floor like some sort of Jedi Knight, cutting through the weirdoes and scam artists with the precision of a surgeon, whilst at the same time enjoying the colour and diversity that they bring to the party.

---

[9] March 2018

Really Clever, 'Scientific Match-making' Sites

Finally, we come to my favourite flavour of dating site. Those that do slightly more than take your money, personal details, and then throw you to the wolves.

In a world where virtually everybody is connected by little boxes, each of which have more computing power than NASA used to put a man on the moon, it's staggering that most dating websites do nothing more than allow you to 'search profiles' and 'send messages'. Wow. Is that it? I mean, I can accept the fact that there isn't a moon base, teleportation or flying cars, but for the love of all that's holy you'd think by now we'd have managed to evolve a better way of matching people's romantic needs than merely putting them together in an enclosed space, virtual or otherwise, and hoping that everyone figures it out!

Maybe we have.

There are a handful of sites that are prepared to have a pretty good stab at giving Cupid more than a cheap bow and arrow to find his mark. Let's have a quick look at some of them:

Three 'Clever' Sites

Whilst there are others, three of the most popular dating sites that also do a degree of clever 'matching stuff' are *eHarmony*, *Parship*, and *OKCupid*[10].

eHarmony[11]

eHarmony is arguably the most famous of the 'clever' sites. Like many of these sites you have to spend about half an hour answering initial questions before you're allowed 'in'. These are less 'relationship based' than you might expect, and more about your personality and attitude to life. The majority are along the lines of "how well do the following words sum you up?". To answer you simply click somewhere on a ten-point scale.

At the end of all this questioning *eHarmony* generate a rather interesting character analysis report. You can find mine on my website[12]. I can't vouch for anyone else's experience, but my report is spookily accurate.

Once you're up and running you're presented with more questions such as:

- The one thing I am most passionate about…
- The most important thing I am looking for in a person is…
- Three of my best life-skills are…
- The first thing people notice about me is…

---

[10] I'm not affiliated with any of the sites mentioned in this book. I haven't used them all (!!!) and their inclusion shouldn't be considered an endorsement of any kind.

[11] This information based on my own research which was, admittedly, back in December 2012.

[12] *HowToStopWaitingAndStartDating.com*

It's these questions that make up your 'profile text', which makes controlling your profile both easy, *and* a challenge, depending on how you look at it.

But the questioning doesn't stop there. Each and every time you look at someone's profile *eHarmony* says something like "this person answered these questions. Why don't you?" This is a nice touch. It makes you feel like you're getting to know the person you're looking at, and that, in my opinion, is one of *eHarmony*'s strengths. They're big on their 'guided communication'.

One of the problems with regular dating sites is that someone usually has to make 'the first move' – *eHarmony* attempts to resolve this by taking you through their five 'guided communication stages' – which are; 'get to know each other', 'must haves and can't stands', 'learn more', and '*eHarmony* mail'

For instance, during the 'getting to know each other' stage you select five relationship multi-choice style questions from a list that you'd like the person you're looking at to answer. Much better than a 'wave' or a 'wink'. Easier than composing a 'message'. Does it work? Possibly. Probably. To find out involves signing up for a membership (which I haven't done) but it's worth pointing out that you can get to this stage without parting with any money at all.

'Parting with money' is also the only way to see anyone's photos, which, as we'll discuss later in the book, is a big deal for me. And whilst we're discussing 'big deals', *eHarmony* put quite a lot on emphasis on the 'basic information' – how much you earn, what level of education you achieved, etc – which, depending on your personal level of 'hippyness', may or may not be important to you.

There's also no kind of 'match' score.

Sure, *eHarmony* presents you with a list of people whom it thinks you're compatible with – in my case just one person! (Hello 'Kerry from Kent') – but there's no way of telling just how well matched you actually are. Does *eHarmony* consider Kerry and I soulmates? Or are we the last two people left after everyone else was paired off? You might laugh, but the next two sites we're going to look at can tell you *exactly* this kind of information.

Parship

Parship also makes you answer a bunch of personality questions before you can do anything else. Amongst them there are some intriguing questions based around abstract images, which gives the impression that these people really know their stuff.

However, most of the questions assume that you're monogamous, and ultimately looking for marriage. In fact, whilst they're busy interrogating you, *Parship*'s questions actually reveal quite a lot about its creators and what their site is ultimately about. If you'd happily skip this dating stage and move directly to marriage, followed by a life-long traditional relationship living under the same roof, *Parship* is probably the site for you. If, on the other hand, you're looking for something slightly different, or your views on relationships are a little more 'out there', *Parship* might feel a little conservative for your liking, and answering their questions a little like trying to fit a square peg into a round hole.

What *Parship* does give you, however, is a 'compatibility score'. At one glance you can tell just how compatible you are with someone else, and this, in my opinion, is online dating *gold*.

In *Parship*'s case the compatibility score is always between 60 and 140 points. A score of 100 points is considered as average. A score of 110 or more is exceptional. Given my slightly liberal nature however, you can probably guess how many matches I had in this range.

OKCupid

Ah, *OKCupid*. How I love thee. Shall I count the ways?

I probably ought to come clean right now. Back when I was an 'active dater' *OKCupid* was my favourite online dating site. I'm not affiliated with it in any way, it just worked for me. But I am the first to admit it's not for everyone.

For starters, whilst the structure of sites such as *eHarmony* and *Parship* weed out the majority of scammers, spammers, and anyone less than serious about dating – *OKCupid* is free and easy to join. This sometimes means they have more than their fair share of web-based hoodlums – though the moderators are pretty good at killing them off once they've been flagged.

Also, whilst *eHarmony* and *Parship* grill all new members rigorously before a dating profile is created, *OKCupid*'s very laid back about the whole personality profiling thing. Consequently, those 'clever' scores don't necessarily work all of the time.

But here's what *OKCupid* has got going for it.

It too has questions. Millions of them. And they are – in my humble if slightly biased opinion – far more interesting. Why would I say such a thing? Because very few are actually written by the staff of OKC or any 'relationship experts'. They're nearly *all* devised by the members.

You, as a user, answer whichever of these questions you like the look of, *twice* – once for yourself, and once as your ideal person would answer it. You also rate the question's importance. For instance, you might rate a question about your sexual preference as 'very important', whilst a question about your feelings on flag burning might be pretty much 'irrelevant' to you.

The answers you give allow *OKCupid* to generate two compatibility scores – a match score, and an enemy score. From the moment you start answering questions you're able, at a glance, to assess just how compatible you are with almost anyone else on the site. And the more questions you, and everyone else, answers, more accurate those scores become.

But there's more to *OKCupid* than match scores and questions.

If you're a fan of *Tinder,* and all that swiping photos left or right nonsense really appeals to you, then you might be interested to know that *OKCupid* has it's own version called 'Double Take'. Though <u>unlike</u> *Tinder,* you should have MUCH more in common with the people you're presented with than mere geographical location.

Are you a fan of *Facebook*? Then you should have no problem with *OKCupid's* LIKE button. You can LIKE peoples photos, or their profile summary text, or the questions they answer – whatever! *Unlike* the *Facebook* LIKE however, it's not quite as public a declaration of appreciation as you'd think it might be; nobody else can see your 'stamps of approval' – only you and the intended recipient – and even then it's not some sort of cheesy 'virtual wink' or meaningless 'cyber wave'. LIKEs give *OKCupid* more data to work with, and on this site, that's no bad thing.

Fed up with the sheer amount of daily messages from creepy men? *OKCupid* has that covered too; initial messages never appear in your 'conversations' (ongoing messages) *unless* you reply to them. Instead, initial messages are kind of 'attached' to a persons profile, which you'll never see *unless* you like each other and/or share a high match score. This way, if you're a woman, you're not going to be inundated with a million messages, and if you're a nice fella, your message is less likely to be lost in a sea of dross! This alone is a HUGE win over other sites / apps.

Finally by signing up to *OKCupid's* A-list you have access to a whole bunch of sophisticated tools to either help you hunt down that elusive perfect mate, or stand-out amongst the crowd.

It's fair to say that *OKCupid* are really big on technology. And numbers. Which isn't really surprising as several of the site's founders have impressive qualifications in mathematics, and extensive experience in web design and computer science. And yet oddly, amongst their key staff members there doesn't appear to be a single 'relationship guru' – thank the gods! Cupid it seems, gave up that bow and arrow stuff long ago in favour of a kick-ass webserver and lines of computer code.

This kind of technology-rich scientific approach of using numbers and statistics to determine how compatible you are with someone, followed by a creative use of the latest technology to introduce the two of you, really *really* appeals to me. That and the fact it has about a zillion members worldwide. And a pretty groovy laid back liberal feel about it.

As *OKCupid* say themselves, their site is about substance, not (just) selfies.

Staying Anonymous

Back in the days before I transformed into the mild mannered author I am today, I worked as a consultant in the banking industry. Banks are, as a rule, austere places of employment. Fun and frivolity are frowned upon. You're allowed to have a private life – of course – in the sense that they accept you've got to be somewhere when you're not at the bank, but in truth banks would probably prefer it if their employees didn't leave the building.

At that time, I'd recently made the decision to start dating again after the death of my wife. I created a profile on one of the more popular world-wide dating websites, and whilst it wasn't a secret – friends and colleagues knew that I was dating – I naively assumed the only people who'd be interested in viewing it would be women of a similar mindset. How wrong I was.

One evening, on returning from a client, I logged into my dating account only to discover that there, in the list of people who'd recently viewed my profile, was the photo of a fairly senior bank manager who I'd been working with earlier that day. This was a lady whom I was relatively certain was not the slightest bit interested in forming a romantic relationship with me – after years of therapy and soul-searching I'd finally come to accept that I *might* not be a bad looking bloke, that ladies *might* want to spend some time in my company, but to this day I steadfastly refuse to believe I can turn a gay woman straight. Call me paranoid and egocentric, but I came to the swift conclusion that the only reason she was on the site and looking at my profile, was sheer bloody nosiness.

I deleted my account. Immediately.

Less than twenty four hours later my assumptions were confirmed when a colleague, who worked for said manager, asked me why I'd taken down my profile.

We live in an increasingly virtual world, where privacy is not only hard to enforce, but pretty much impossible. When it comes to online dating it's a challenge to strike a balance between being open, honest and available to people who might find you attractive, and compromising your day-to-day life.

There might be numerous reasons why you want to retain some anonymity. Perhaps you're the head of a global corporation and you'd rather not risk your staff seeing your cuddly, cute romantic side. Or perhaps you and your partner have a relaxed and enlightened view of matrimony that your traditional churchgoing family would struggle to accept. Maybe you're a teacher and you don't want your pupils delving into your private life. Or perhaps you're Kylie Minogue, and you need to be sure that any potential suitor is attracted to you for your charm and lovely demeanor, rather than your money and fame (may I just take this opportunity to point out Miss Minogue, that I am indeed *that* man).

I'm not going to debate the ethics of why you might want to remain anonymous – you'll have your reasons – but if it's important to you here are a few things to consider:

The internet is as local as it is global.

Modern dating sites are designed to allow members to search for people *locally*. In the next chapter I'll give you good reasons why you might want to pick your nearest city as your location, rather than your home town, but if anonymity is an issue to you this could be one way to *reduce* the chances of being 'found' by your neighbours.

Limit the potential damage.

Minimise the damage of being discovered by being very careful with what you put on your profile. Assume that everything – photos and text – will immediately be made public the moment you're recognised. Using those pictures of you in that saucy Little Bo Peep outfit might not be a wise move.

Stay in the shadows.

Avoid the free sites. You're less likely to be found on a site where someone has to part with money to look at profiles. Also, consider picking a site that blurs your photo by default, and allows you to choose who gets to see it. If your site doesn't blur photos, check the options to see if you can restrict your profile to paid-up members only.

"Why am I here? Why are you here?"

A risky strategy, but one that might work, might be to pick a site where a fellow member would be equally compromised should they decide to 'out' you. From this perspective, *CheatingSpouses.com*[13] might actually be the way to go.

Don't invite trouble.

Whilst there's no shame in online dating, if you want to remain anonymous tell only your nearest and dearest of your online dating exploits. Even then, it's prudent to be extremely absent minded when it comes to remembering the name of your dating site of choice. Lie if you have to. When someone comes back to you and says "It's weird, I couldn't find your profile on *DatingWorld.com*" you'll thank me.

Check the small print.

In the terms and conditions of your chosen website, check for any clauses that talk about "reserving the right to use your image for advertising purposes". You want to avoid your face appearing on a billboard, a TV advertisement, or more likely, in a mass email campaign. Some sites allow you to opt out of this, others don't.

---

[13] Made up site. Real versions do exist.

Use different pictures.

Do not use pictures that you've ever uploaded anywhere else, or ever sent to someone via email. This includes similar looking pictures. Take completely new photos specifically for your dating profile. This'll reduce the chances of your profile being found should someone perform a 'reverse image search'.

Get a wide brimmed hat.

Whilst you're taking new pictures, find ingenious ways to disguise your photos or mask your face. Throw your head back, look over your shoulder, happen to be holding the world's largest ice-cream right in front of your face. If at all possible use your desire for anonymity as an opportunity to create some fun, mysterious photos. Don't resort to Photoshop – many sites disallow images that have clearly been tampered with.

Create an element of doubt

Even if your pictures still look like you, you can sometimes introduce an element of doubt into the minds of viewers by ensuring that:

- nothing else on the profile confirms their suspicions (such as a local landmark within the photograph)
- a couple things actually contradict what they know about you.

Pick a username that suggests your name might be Tom, when actually it's Gerald, state your location as London when it's actually Kent.

Your location and username are probably the only details you can 'tweak' without undermining any potential date, but it *might* just be enough to convince someone you know that all they've found is a lookalike.

Monitor your visitors.

Many sites allow you to see who's been looking at your profile. Later in this book, I'll tell you why you shouldn't bother with this facility but if you want to stay anonymous this might be an exception to that rule. Keep an eye on who's watching you, and get ready to hit the delete button the moment you're rumbled.

The pre-emptive strike.

Here's an alternative approach. One way to avoid being outed might be to ignore all of the above advice and out yourself. Tell *everyone* what site you're on and where they can find it. Encourage people to visit and tell you what they think. Chances are no one will bother. The funny thing about secrets, is that people are only interested in them when they're secret!

Is it really an issue?

Finally, if the only reason you don't want to be recognised on a dating site is to avoid the shame of being labeled as some sort of desperate saddo who can't get a girlfriend/boyfriend any other way, let me be the first to shake you by the shoulders and slap you. This is the 21st Century! We read books on portable flat screen devices, carry our entire music collection around in tiny metal boxes, have our groceries delivered, do our banking in the middle of the night, in our jim jams, and if we fail to reply to a text message for a couple of hours our friends and relatives flip out and assume we've been kidnapped. Internet Dating may have evolved from the lonely hearts column of your local paper but it's moved on considerably. It's no longer a 'last resort'. For many it's either the *only* way to meet new people, or their preferred way, and anyone who tells you anything different is an out-of-touch fossil, and ought to be treated as such! Enough with the anonymity – let's take some action!

STOP! ACTION POINT!

Choose a Dating Website

Things to bear in mind:

- I can pretty much guarantee this won't be your last online dating site. Think of it like your first car[14]. With this in mind DON'T sign up for a twelve month deal. You want the option to move somewhere else when you've learnt more.
- Consider the recommendations of friends.
- Browse a handful of sites but don't go overboard – pick the first one you like the look of.
- Consider signing up to more than one site.
- For now just choose your site – hold fire on joining and creating a profile. We'll do that together in a page or two.

---

[14] If you don't drive or you still own your first car, please pick a different analogy.

BUILDING A DATING PROFILE

Having decided on your dating website of choice, it's time to take the plunge. Clear an hour or two, or set aside an evening (yes, you'll probably need that long), sit yourself down at your computer, and open a blank *Word* document, or something similar.

Hold up – you might be asking yourself – why aren't we logging into the website and filling in the blanks?

Oh we will, I promise you, but before we do that you need to write your *self-summary*.

Writing Your Self Summary

After your photos, the most important thing on your dating profile, and to a lesser extent social media, are the words, and the order you choose to put them in.

Even if you've decided to use a dating site or app such as *Tinder*, which is happy for you to build a profile with nothing but photos, any text you add or could add is still important – in fact, I'd argue it's more important than ever, because it's an opportunity to stand out from the crowd and show folks that you're far more than just a pretty face. Trust me. You'll thank me later.

As you can probably tell, I'm a big fan of words. You can change the world with words. At least, theoretically. You can certainly change someone's mind, and when it comes to using the internet to attract a potential date, what we want are words that infuse your online profile with your personality, and how you are on a really, really good day.

I'm talking here about your *self summary*, and any other section where you describe yourself or what you're looking for.

Almost everyone hates this bit. It's a rare person who can sit down and with very little effort paint a flattering, yet self-deprecating, portrait of themselves in words. And, faced with this kind of pressure, many, *many* people, choose to start their self summary by telling the reader how much they *hate* writing self-summaries. Some even attempt to side-step the self-summary issue entirely by inviting the reader to ask them questions. "I'll tell you anything you want to know," they offer cheerfully, which is both an outright lie and an invitation for all kinds of unwanted solicitations. Finally, there are those who, with half-hearted optimism, complete each box with the words 'I'll fill this in later'. Which of course they never will.

We – you and I – are not going to be those people.

Other things we're not going to do include these popular, but highly questionable, self-summary approaches:

- Mentioning past or failed relationships

- Talking about how lonely we've been

- Making pointed remarks about how there seem to be nothing but idiots on dating sites

- Cataloguing our dating disasters

- Listing our hatred of dating, dating sites, people on dating sites, the way people use dating sites, or anything similar.

- Beginning our profile with a list of must-have criteria, and/or threats if someone fails to comply

What you *are* going to do is *charm*. You're going to flirt, you're going to be nice, you're going to be funny. You're basically going to be so goddamn attractive that having flagged down a passing potential-suitor with your lead picture, and kept them around with your remaining photos, any reservations they may have had about contacting you will instantly evaporate in the presence of your sizzling wit.

Basically, you're going to *sell*!

Now I don't know about you, but I've never been much of a salesperson. To me 'sales' always seems kind of 'sordid'. It feels one-step removed from lying. If I have to sell something, then really, it can't be that great. Can it?

Like a lot of men I'd rather deal in facts. Explain what my product – in this case, me – has got going for it, and let the 'buyer' make an informed decision.

Unfortunately, that doesn't actually work.

At least, not well.

People are rubbish at making decisions based on facts. Most people rely wholly and solely on their gut instincts. Their feelings. Which actually, when it comes to affairs of the heart is a very, very good thing.

'Feelings' are what relationships are all about. Regardless of how and why a relationship starts, we stick around because of how that person makes us feel. And if those feelings change the relationship changes. Any so-called facts – that a person is the right height, right age, has the right body shape, has the right taste in music, drives the right car – are actually irrelevant.

Grab your mouse

Writing your profile text, and getting it right, takes a while. It's also something that you'll probably come back to again and again to update and tweak. And, should you ever decide to make the move from *SinfulLovers.com* to *SecondTimeAround.co.uk*, it might need a complete overhaul. With this in mind, write your profile in *Word*, or *Notepad*, or some other text editor on your computer or gadget of choice, and cut and paste it into the website when the time comes.

All writers know that there are few things more terrifying than a blank page, so open the wish-list you created back at the start of the book – the one where you imagined the sort of person you're looking for – and described the sorts of things the two of you would get up to. This task will be a whole lot easier with that to refer to. You might even be able to copy and paste elements you've already written.

The opening

There are many ways you could start your self-summary. Personally, I like to open with a series of quick-fire summary sentences describing the sort of person I am.

You could start with a short physical description. Maybe, "I'm tall, lean and smiley" – or "short, curvy and bubbly" or "above average height, below average waist, rubbish at statistics."

Notice that I've used groups of three. 'Threes' always work well. Think, "friends, Romans, countrymen…"

Notice too, that although we're throwing out 'facts', in reality, we're using it as an excuse to communicate your personality. Don't get hung up on how tall, short, stocky, or lean you *actually* are – think of these words as triggers, firing off emotions in the mind of your reader.

Whilst we're discussing words, steer clear of telling the world you're 'attractive'. It's such an overused word that it's virtually meaningless, bordering on annoying. Let's start from the assumption that you are an outstanding specimen of humanity.

Men – unless you're going to be using a site with a strong sexual bias try to avoid describing anything below your waistline, no matter how blessed you may be. And you know what, even if you *are* on a site with a sexual bias, why not be the one guy who doesn't mention his genitalia! Hey, now there's a wacky idea.

If you're a transvestite, or transgendered, or in any way born the opposite gender from the one you've selected on your profile, this would be the moment to mention it. Likewise, this is a good time to mention if you're married, non-monogamous, a porn-star, particularly religious, or anything else that tends to polarize opinions. Don't apologise for what you are – be a married, non-monogamous, religious transsexual porn star, and proud! True, not everyone's going to be cool with that, but you'll be surprised how many will be, and it'll avoid a huge amount of potential heartache and hate-mail further down the line.

Here are some particularly strong openers:

I'm a vintage loving, ever-so mischievous, slightly awkward, feminine girl, with a penchant for sun, sea, and sixties music.

Upfront, straight talking lady – looking for my partner in crime; A Clyde to my Bonnie, a Butch to my Sundance.

I'm more of a listener than a talker. Friends describe me as compassionate, thoughtful, and sensitive. They also describe me as quirky, crazy and wonderfully mad.

Curious, contrary and colourful. I'm a passionate chef looking for someone to test my recipes on!

I am very tall. This amuses some people. They say things like "what's the weather like up there?"

Optimistic pessimist. Wannabe geek. Arch-cynicist.

I live between Canvey Island and New York – my heart's in the East Village whilst my books are in a little apartment overlooking the Thames Estuary. My favourite shoes are white Converse trainers. I fantasize about getting a dog. I love paddling in the sea. Sometimes I'm an eccentric dresser. I spend far too much time in book shops.

How you getting on with your opening? Come on – you can read and write at the same time, surely?

If you're struggling, you could focus on what you *do*, rather than what you're like. And when I say 'what you do' I don't necessarily mean what you do for a living – not unless your job involves wearing some kind of uniform (that'll certainly get some attention). No, forget about work, concentrate instead on what you do when you're *not* in the office. What are your passions? What do you enjoy? Travel? Theatre? Sports?

What you're looking for

Your 'opening' can last as long as you like – if the quick fire sentences are working for you, stick with them for a paragraph, maybe two – but at some point you want to shift gear, and start giving your visitor more detail.

This is a good time to start talking about what you're looking for. This should be fairly straightforward if you're referring to that wish list. Take those thoughts and work them into your self-summary. Be bold. Be blatant. Say something like, "I imagine a typical evening might go something like this…" then describe it. In detail.

Your most important tool when writing your profile is 'imagination' – yours and the reader's. You want to create a scene in the reader's head – one with you and them in it. Something exciting, or romantic, or sexy… whatever it is that you're looking for.

Let's try this now: stop for a second and think about how you'd like things to be several weeks from now. You've read this book, followed the advice, your profile was an amazing success, and after a handful of dates you're now seeing someone regularly. What will the two of you be doing together? What is it that you really want?

Got it?

Okay – now write that down.

So for instance, let's say you are looking for a partner to travel the world with. You might describe how you'd love to sit together, hand in hand, and watch the sun fall behind the pyramids, at the end of another hot and humid, but completely fabulous, day.

Keep your descriptions light and breezy. Smile whilst you write them. Fun fun fun. It's no big deal.

Here are some descriptive paragraphs that illustrate my point perfectly.

I should also mention that I'm very excited about the prospect of being able to utter sentences such as; "We're going to New York for the weekend!" and "We're still deciding on a theme for our dinner party," and "We didn't know what to do with all our CDs so we've used them as table legs." I'm pretty confident with 1st-person singular sentences – bored with them in fact – the prospect of forming a sentence structure that suggests a twosome is very attractive.

I find myself almost irresistibly attracted to people who enjoy any or all of the following: being daft a good deal of the time; talking away into the wee small hours; walking barefoot on the sand; grilling fresh mackerel on an empty beach; foraging for wild mushrooms (or whatever happens to be in season right now). Is that you? Can you fill my plate with goodies and my stomach with butterflies?

I want to start each day with a cuddle.... have wild nights out... stay in and nibble cheese and biscuits. I don't need bunches of flowers.... a single rose from the park means more knowing you thought of me when you saw it.

Back to you

At some point, switch back to talking about yourself. In fact, scientists have discovered that you need to talk about yourself roughly *twice as much* as you talk about the sort of person you're looking for[15], so when you're done describing the sun setting behind the pyramids talk about why that's important to you.

Again, let your imagination take control. Get a little more wordy than you might usually allow yourself to be.

Here are a couple of great self-descriptive paragraphs:

> I love the countryside and feel most at peace when sat under a mighty oak, or by a stream. I treat my cats like they are my children, and I'm delighted when they respond in kind. My fondest memories abroad are of summers in the South of France, picnics with my family, and boat trips with friends. I also loved exploring Amsterdam by bike and found the locals to be extremely welcome and friendly.

> I love dining out but also enjoy entertaining from home. I wish more of my friends played poker! I love cycling and free wheeling down long hills. Thunderstorms thrill me, rain calms me. And unusually I'm a girl that likes video games — I'm determined to master all the routines in Dance Nation.

Give your reader something to comment on

The wonderful thing about putting your imagination in the driving seat is that you usually end up writing lots, and giving the reader more to comment on, which is a very, very good thing, and here's why: when it comes to writing that first, opening message it can be

---

[15] In actual fact the ratio should be 70:30 – 70 percent of your profile should talk about you, 30 percent about what you're looking for. Check the website for a blog post on this very topic.

exceptionally hard to know what to say. A smart online-dater will scan through the profile text and look for something they can comment on, or ask about, but you'll be astonished at how few profiles mention anything of any interest.

We don't want your visitors to have that problem. We want to give them plenty to comment on. In fact, we want them to become so enamored and curious about you that they're no longer trying to find some cheesy conversation starter, but genuinely want to know more.

Ask for opinions. Begin a discussion. Say something slightly controversial – anything! Just give your readers lots of reasons to message you.

Be really specific

Try really hard to avoid writing a profile that could apply to anyone. *Everyone* enjoys movies, listening to music, quiet nights in, and the occasional restaurant meal. We want details!

What's your favourite movie of all time? If your MP3 player only had one hour of battery life left before it died for good, what album or song would you listen to? What does a "quiet night in" actually involve? And if you could open a restaurant of your own, what sort of food would it serve?

If you haven't done so already, now would be a good time to mention any interests that are peculiar to you. If you don't have any peculiar interests get some!

Working With Headings

Nobody enjoys writing a profile. Did I mention that already? Because of this, many dating websites have started to experiment with ways of making the task easier, and less daunting. By and large their solutions are usually to break the Self Summary into sections, and either give each section a heading, or make it the answer to a question.

Here are some popular Self-Summary Section Headings or Questions:

- What I'm doing with my life
- I'm really good at…
- The first thing people usually notice about me
- Favourite books / movies / music
- The three things I'm most grateful for
- The six things I can never do without
- I spend a lot of time thinking about…
- On a typical Friday night I am…
- The most private thing I'm willing to admit

The great thing about these type of headings is that they can help generate ideas about what to write about, the lousy thing about headings like this is that they can also box you in and prevent you from writing something that would otherwise be charming, witty and attractive. My advice, therefore, is to cut and paste parts of your self-summary under appropriate headings when they suit, but ignore them completely and write (paste) whatever you want when they don't.

Incidentally, if your website of choice doesn't use headings like this there's nothing to stop you using these for inspiration.

Stay Positive

As if all this wasn't hard enough, it's essential to focus on the positive – what you *want* the reader to feel, not what you *don't* want them to feel.

If, for example, you start talking about how you'd like a better job because the one you have now just sucks the life out of you, and some days you find it hard to summon enough energy to drag yourself out of bed and face another day in the office – your reader will start to imagine those things. The life will seep out of them. Their mood will darken.

One of two things will happen at this point; they'll either move on to another profile – one that makes them feel happier. Or they might contact you – meaning that you've just managed to attract someone who feels more comfortable with negative feelings. Not the best start to a relationship, I'm sure you'll agree.

Words like 'don't' 'not' 'mustn't' really have no place in your self-summary. Stay positive. Concentrate on what you want.

Encourage photos

Many, many people end their self-summaries with the words "no photo – no reply". There's no need to be quite so blunt (or negative) but words to a similar effect might not be a bad idea. I myself have used the following postscript:

> Messages from ladies in or around London,
> with profiles that contain both words
> AND full length photos (of you)
> are sure to get my attention.
> Other profiles... mmmm, not so much.

This has always worked well for me. It's fun, a little cheeky, but makes it pretty clear who can and can't expect a reply.

How much should you write?

Brevity has always been a challenge for me. My self-summary was over a thousand words long. But that's okay. On *most* sites there isn't an upper limit. There is however a little known *lower* limit.

Research[16] shows that men need to pen 130 words or more – presumably just enough to prove that they have a brain. Women on the other hand need to write much, much more. Statistically, female self-summaries of 800 words or more do much better than the average length of 280.

Which is a problem if you're using *Tinder*.

---

[16] Check the website for a list of citations.

Tinder

Whilst *Tinder* is all about pictures, it too allows you to add a short Self Summary which appears when someone decides to look at your additional photos.

Because most *Tinder* users don't bother writing a Self Summary, using it will actually give you something of an edge and, if my experience in anything to go by, dramatically improve your chances of meeting someone who you might be compatible with.

There is however one huge fly in the ointment. For reasons best known to *Tinder*, there's a ridiculous 500 character limit. That's barely a hundred words – which as you've just read, is not quite enough for men, and woefully inadequate for women.

However, if that's all we've got to play with, then we're going to use it! Take the long version of your profile text – the one you've been writing during this chapter – save it in case you need to come back to it, then create a *cut down Tinder* version keeping all the funny charming bits that show what a lovely person you are.

Phew! Let's summarise all that.

STOP! ACTION POINT!

Write your profile text

- Write and save your profile in *Word* or some other text editor on your computer.

- Engage your imagination!

-Start with some quick, quirky, self-descriptions that communicate your personality.

- Move on to what you want, but concentrate on how the other person will make you feel.

- Remember to talk about yourself roughly twice as much as the person you're looking for.

- Give the reader plenty to comment on.

- Stay positive!

- Write lots! Men need at least 130 words, whereas women should top 800 if possible.

- *Tinder* has a 500 character limit – 100 words approx. Use them anyway, it'll help you to stand out from the crowd.

Your Basic Information

Most websites and apps usually ask you to specify whether you're male or female, how old you are, where in the world you live, and the sex of your preferred date, as well as a plethora of other information that is, as we discussed earlier, pretty much meaningless when it comes to a successful romance.

This is usually referred to as the 'basic information', and its only purpose is usually to give members something to search on – which means that whatever you provide under 'basic information' could determine whether or not you'll be discovered when another member conducts a 'search'. With this in mind you might want to consider very carefully how accurate your basic information is. For instance, there are some things – such as your marital status, your actual gender (rather than the gender you'd like to be) and whether you're a full-time parent – where I'd recommend being brutally honest, but the rest isn't nearly so cut and dried, and there are at least three pieces of information where it's almost essential *that you lie*.

Your Username

Most sites require you to come up with a username – a catchy 'handle' or nickname which other members will address you by. Generally speaking, the site will require this to be unique (different from every other member) and quite often your username can never be changed.

Despite these restrictions, a large number of users will blithely type in their first name, and when the site tells them that the username 'Sarah' has already been taken they'll add their surname and try again. If the online dating gods are watching, hopefully 'SarahSmith' – or any similar variations – will also have been taken, but if Sarah is determined she'll simply start adding numbers at the end of her username, numbers that she's likely to remember. Eventually "sarahsmith1973" is created.

You might be tempted to do the same.

Don't be.

To do so would be revealing information that could be used, by nefarious individuals, to track down your address or access other online accounts you might hold (including bank accounts). I'd like to introduce you to the first Golden Rule of Dating.

DATING GOLDEN RULE #1:

NEVER REVEAL INFORMATION TO WEBSITES
THAT COULD ASSIST SCAMMERS, SPAMMERS, OR FRAUDSTERS
(UNLESS DOING SO WOULD PREVENT THE WEBSITE
FROM WORKING PROPERLY).

Personal safety aside, you're actually missing an opportunity to reveal an aspect of your personality that might make you irresistible to potential dates. If you're a humorous person, pick a username that reflects your sparkling wit. If you're a dog lover, pick a dog-related handle. If all else fails, take a look around you and create a username based on the first object you lay your eyes on.

Interestingly, there's some research that suggests that usernames that start with a letter nearer the beginning of the alphabet do better than usernames that don't. So *Albus Dumbledore* might be a better choice of username than *Zaphod Beeblebrox*.

Why should this be?

I suspect it's because computers like to sort lists, and in the absence of any other criteria they'll default to either a numerical sort, or an alphabetical one. Meaning that if *Albus* and *Zaphod* were to be amongst the same set of search results, there's a good chance *Albus* would pip *Zaphod* to the number one slot.

Your Password

When it comes to picking a password it makes sense to be even more cautious. Avoid, if you can, using the same password you may have used on other dating sites, or worse still your email account or banking website – especially if your password is nothing more complicated than the name of your cat with the number one following it!

Whilst you might think your password is pretty difficult to guess, most fraudsters worth their evil-salt are armed with software that can crack the average password in milliseconds.

A good password should be made up words or a nonsensical stream of at least eight characters. They should contain both upper and lower case letters, numbers, *and* a special character or two. G3rr@1d would make a good password – and all I did there was take the name Gerald, added an extra R, and swapped a few letters for numbers or symbols.

If remembering usernames and passwords is a pain, take a look at *SplashID* or other similar software. It's a 'password safe' – somewhere to store all your usernames and passwords, and other sensitive information. It'll even synchronize and backup to your phone so that you'll never lose or be without that information.

If all this talk of fraud and security sounds a little paranoid consider this: I once had my credit cards compromised merely because I used to be in the habit of using the same username and password on every website that insisted I create an account. It was only a matter of time before someone – someone who's online store I'd visited and used – decided to see if the username and password I'd created for their site could be used elsewhere. Boy howdy did I learn that lesson the hard way! So be smart. Keep security-related information to yourself whenever and wherever you can.

Your real name

Some sites insist you provide your real name, though they promise this information will never be revealed to the real world. Once again, unless they need this information to process your credit card payment, make something up. They're only asking so that they can personalize any emails they send to you. But you have no idea who at the dating site is going to see that information.

Your Date of Birth

Never *ever* use your real birth *day*. As date-of-birth is used as a security question for many financial organisations, for your own safety it's best not to divulge this information[17]. If you really don't want to lie about your age then make yourself one or two days older.

There is another reason why you might want to change your date-of-birth. List your age as 41, and people searching for partners in the 30-40 age bracket won't find you. List your age as 39 and people searching for partners in the 40-50 age bracket won't find you. If you're hoping to be found by someone more mature or young at heart, and don't want to be excluded by their ridiculous search criteria (after all, not everyone has had the benefit of reading this book) then a little age adjustment might be in order.

If you're using *Tinder*, or plan to, then changing your age is a tad more complex than simply typing in your date of birth.

Tinder pulls all it's 'basic information' from *Facebook* as you install the app and start it for the first time – *so before you do that*, change your date of birth on *Facebook*. You can correct *Facebook* later without *Tinder* being affected.

If you've *already* downloaded *Tinder* and want to change your age, you'll need to delete the app from your device, change your date of birth on *Facebook*, and then re-download and re-install *Tinder*. You can then change your date of birth (on *Facebook*) back to what it was originally.

Your location

Way back in the mists of time, when I first experimented with online dating, I discovered a curious thing. There were, according to *Match.com* (one of only six dating websites that were around back then) about three women in the South East of England. I wasn't really surprised, it was the general lack of single females that had

---

[17] Regardless of what a site might lead you to believe, date-of-birth is not required to authorise a credit card payment, so providing a false date-of-birth will *not* cause your payment to be declined.

brought me to online dating in the first place, so to be told that there were only three of them within any kind of distance that didn't require a day's travelling was merely confirmation that I'd left it far too late to get hitched.

But that wasn't the reason.

There were plenty of single women – but back then your average single lady was unlikely to be a paid-up member of *Match.com* – hell, she was unlikely to have a computer.

These days, everyone's connected to the net, and, contrary to what you might think, the stigma of online dating has virtually vanished. And yet, until comparatively recently, I was still dumfounded by how few 'available' people there seemed to be in my local area. Or at least I was, until I compared how many there were in my nearest *city*.

To demonstrate my point, if you happen to be close to an internet enabled device, log on to the website craigslist (.co.uk or .com) and pick your nearest major city from the right hand column (for me it would be London). Click on the category under the heading 'personals', and count up the number of ads you see there for a typical day. Now go back to craigslist home page, click on a smaller town or county (perhaps the one where you live, if it's listed – for me it would be Essex, for you it might be Kent), and do the same again. You should notice significantly less ads, *even* if the county or town you selected actually covers a bigger area than the city.

There are several reasons for this. Firstly, cities are far, far more densely populated. Secondly, the lifestyle of people living in cities is very different to that of people living in towns. By and large, the average age of a city's population is younger, and the percentage of single people significantly higher. Thirdly, a whole load of people from the towns and outlying districts commute into the cities on a daily basis and having made the trek, often stay there to socialise. Many of those people will consider that their primary hunting ground for romance – if they're using an online dating site they'll search for people in their city of choice, and they'll list themselves as living in that city so that they too can be 'hunted'.

When I'd finally figured this out and changed my 'home' from Essex to London it was like I'd been standing in the hallway at a house-party with two or three rather dull people, only to find about fifty people in the lounge all having a great time. But, more than that, I started to meet ladies who were doing exactly the same as me. I estimate only fifty per cent of the ladies I've ever met from online dating actually live in London – most, like me, live just outside.

There are two obvious down sides to lying about where you live and picking your nearest city as your location. Firstly, you've just lied – and that undermines your integrity somewhat. But we can fix that. Secondly, though, you may have to travel into the city to do your dating, and that could make your dating exploits more expensive, and time consuming. But, by the same token, it might also make your dating more exciting, and more interesting. And it's certainly worth it.

When I talk to people about their online dating experiences, those that struggle to find anyone to date invariably list their 'location' as their *home town* (as you would), and are consequently fishing in a very small pond. Of all the ideas in this book, this is probably the 'quickest win' there is.

Unless you actually live in a major city your first 'legitimate lie' should be your location. In order to increase the number of potential dates pick your closest city, and not your actual home town or county. By default *Tinder* uses your current location. You can swipe in other locations, but only if you're happy to upgrade.

Warning. Very, very occasionally you'll come across a dating website that asks for your postcode. Usually, they're just doing this so that they can show your location on a map, or notify you of other members living locally – they're not going to send you any snail-mail, and it's not needed for payment processing. However, a postcode can be pretty specific and in these days of identity theft it's not wise to give out this information unless absolutely necessary. Even if you are a city dweller, it's probably wise to use *Google* Maps to find an alternative postcode to give them.

'Un-lying'

Once you're past the opening few words in your self-summary text you might want to squeeze in a line to correct any un-truths you might have told in your basic information.

For instance, if you're a year or two older than the date of birth in your 'basic information' make a joke about it in the self-summary, and state your real age. If you live outside the city you've claimed as your home town, add the words "I live just a few miles outside…".

There's no need to make a big deal about it or go into long, rambling explanations. Sentences that start "I've lied in my basic information because…" are not the way to go. Just clarify exactly how old you are and the general area you live, and then move on.

Building a *Tinder* Profile

I'm not really a fan of *Tinder*. There. I've said it. It has the *potential* to be an awesome dating app, but instead it feels like the virtual equivalent of a rather grubby night club. In fact, living as I do in Essex, most of the photos I'm presented with (from which I'm supposed to choose a potential suitor) are of drunken girls in grubby nightclubs! Often these girls are in groups, meaning it's virtually impossible to know who's profile I'm actually looking at. A few words in the *Self Summary* along the lines of "I'm the girl in the red dress" might help – but no one ever writes a *Self Summary* on *Tinder*. Then again, a lot of those girls kind of look the same, so does it really matter? It's like picking a Barbie doll off a production line.

All of which is a roundabout way of saying that a few minutes spent building a great *Tinder* profile will pay *significant* dividends.

So, pick some great photos, write a stunning *Self Summary*, and prepare to leave those boring night club girls and guys behind.

Signing Up

So, you know that feeling when you've been rehearsing for weeks and weeks and weeks... That feeling when you've had fifteen bazillion driving lessons, or you've been tossing a contract back and forth for so long there doesn't seem to be a punctuation mark that hasn't been argued about, or you know the telephone numbers of the estate agent and/or the solicitor by heart simply because you never seem to call anyone else? That feeling when you desperately want this part of your life to end and the next part of your life to start? You know that feeling? Well, congratulations. Today's the day. Today, you finally get to sign-up to an online dating website.

Sit yourself in front of your computer, or grab your phone or tablet, and using everything we've prepared in the previous few chapters... sign up! Here are TWO handy Action Points. Pick the one appropriate to you.

STOP! ACTION POINT!

Signing-up to a dating site / app (that ISN'T Tinder)!

Remember the following:

- Paid sites: never sign up for a 12 month membership right off the bat. Sign up for a month / two (three at the very most).
- Think of a clever username that reflects an aspect of your charming personality.
- Create a fabulously complicated password – but one that you can remember.
- Never give the site your real name or postcode – they don't need it.
- Add a day or two to your birthday. Consider adding or subtracting a year or two.
- Pick your nearest city as your home location.
- Complete the basic information.
- Upload your photos.
- Cut and paste your self-summary text.
- Un-lie in the opening paragraph.

STOP! ACTION POINT!

Signing-up to Tinder!

First sign into *Facebook* and:

- Change your age.
- Maybe change your name!
- Upload your photos.

Then:

- Download the *Tinder* App.
- Follow the instructions.
- Select your photos.
- Cut and paste your self-summary text.

THE SEARCH BEGINS

So, using a combination of hard work, preparation, science and technology you should now have a dating profile that presents you in the best light possible.

Make no bones about it, this is an important step forwards.

A duff dating profile – lousy pictures, boring text – will severely hinder your chances of receiving a reply to any messages you might send, and quite aside from the fact you'll be wasting time (and possibly money), you'll also remain single for a good deal longer.

A really good profile, on the other hand, can work wonders, and might actually do much of the 'work' – work that we're going to discuss in this chapter – for you. With a bit of luck *you won't even need this chapter*. It'll simply be a case of logging in to browse your messages and taking your pick from the lovely people who contact you! *If* this happens, (or if messages have *already* started to appear in your inbox), <u>skip ahead</u> to the next chapter ('Reviewing Profiles'), and then again to the one on 'Replying To Messages'. You can always pop back here later when and if you need to.

For the rest of us mere mortals it's important to realise that creating your profile, though important, was just the first step – akin to putting on your 'lucky pants' before setting off to a party. What I need to teach you now is how to 'work the room'.

Important Note: Most of this chapter assumes you're using a regular dating site, but if you've decided to go with *Tinder*, jump forward to the end where there's a special 'browsing basics' section just for you.

How Dating Sites Should Work vs Reality

Remember I mentioned how I used to work in Banking? I'd spend my days hanging around plush corporate offices, the sorts of places where cheesy, motivational pictures hang on every wall; pictures of beautiful people running on beaches, or tiger cubs cavorting in the sun. I remember one photo of a particularly beautiful seascape, the sun setting behind the horizon, and a lone boat just in front of it. The caption read "Don't wait for your ship to come in. Swim out to meet it."

Now, when it comes to ships, I suspect this might be rubbish advice, but when it comes to online dating, well, it's usually the only way. If you're not already getting the number, or the quality of messages you would like, from people you'd like to date, then you need to go in search of those people.

The fundamental concept behind most dating sites is pretty simple, some would say 'dull'. They are nothing more than a platform for people to browse profiles and send each other messages.

In an ideal world, this is what happens:

You receive a message, or decide to send one. Half a dozen exchanges fly back and forth until the two of you arrange to meet. And when you do it feels like you're two old friends catching up on old times. Romance follows.

That's not what happens.

The reality is often similar to the following scenario:

How Dating Sites <u>Really</u> Work

You wait patiently for someone to find your profile and send you a message. *No one does.* In the meantime, you perform numerous 'searches' with an ever broadening criteria and after some extensive browsing you find someone who doesn't repel you. Too much. You spend ages crafting an opening message, and then send it. You wait.

Days. Still no response. Eventually, you phone your internet service provider / local PC repair shop / your techie mate to find out if there's a chance your computer might not be working, or whether there's a problem with the internet, or some other reason why you haven't had a reply. You send a second message enquiring as to whether they got the first. Then, days later, just before you descend into a drunken pit of self-loathing, you come to the inescapable conclusion that they haven't replied because they *didn't like the look of you.*

I don't really want to go into what happens after that – it's usually not good.

Fortunately, my aim in this, and the following sections of this book, is to help you avoid such pitfalls. Doing so isn't necessarily difficult, but, like most things in life, the reality of online dating is significantly more complex than it initially seems.

Take the scenario above. There could be any number of reasons why the other person didn't reply to your message. If I had to put money on it I'd guess that the dating profile you found is *dormant*. Most online dating sites are stuffed full of old abandoned profiles. Your message, and its follow up, are two of many, many messages, that will never be read.

But let's assume, for a moment, that this wasn't the case – that you were smart enough to pick a profile from an active user, and that your message *was* read. In this case, the second most probable reason that you never got a reply is that your message simply failed to make an impression when compared with all the other messages the object of your desire received. And, if you happen to be messaging a particularly attractive person (and this goes double if you're trying to message an attractive *woman*, and double again if she's under the age of forty) your message could be one of dozens sitting in their inbox. Perhaps even *hundreds*. Really. Anyone who gets that many messages soon learns that they can't possibly reply to them all.

What then is the solution? Is there one?

Of course there is. And as with most things in the online dating world, there's an effective way of doing something, and there's the heartbreaking, crazy-making, hair-pulling, frustrating way of doing something.

Lets get you doing the former.

The Browsing Basics

If you've decided to use *Tinder*, jump forward to the next section entitled *Browsing Basics... on Tinder.*

For the rest of you, let's go invisible!

Go invisible

'Browsing' (the act of looking at profiles) is an odd concept. In real life, we quickly learn that it's not polite to stare at people we find attractive. Not when there's a possibility that they might notice. So we develop ways of taking the odd furtive glance at someone who's caught our eye. Online, however, we're actively encouraged to gawp and be gawped at. And yet, people can still react quite badly.

Many dating websites give you the ability to see who's been looking at your profile. Sometimes it appears in the sidebar, other times it's a section on the 'home' page when you log in, occasionally it's a menu item.

Log on to your website of choice and see whether you have such an option. Go ahead. I'll wait.

If you've found it there's a good chance that buried within your profile settings is an option that enables you to 'browse anonymously'. Put simply, 'check' that box and no one will ever know that you've looked at their profile. It's like becoming invisible. You can move amongst the profiles, staring and gawping to your hearts content, and no one will be any the wiser. You'll still show up in searches. People will still find your profile, read it and send you messages. But they won't be able to see how many times you've looked them up and down.

The so-called 'penalty' of ticking this box is that the site will remove your ability to see whose been checking you out. Believe it or not, that's no bad thing.

There are two groups of people who react badly to having their profile looked at.

The first are the 'stalker phobic' folks that consider anyone looking at their profile more than once (the profile that they built and put on a public forum!) some sort of privacy violation. One lady I know describes it as 'lurking', as if she's being peered at from the shadows by unseen predators. It's not lurking. It's looking. It's how online dating works – but you won't convince her or those like her.

Worse still, these people tend to be a little hot headed. They might flag your profile to the site's moderators (who will probably ignore it, but why take the risk), or more likely send you a nasty message telling you to "stop lookin' at my profile u creep." How do I know? Because I've had such messages. Well one. And it really wasn't that aggressive. And I did turn it around by writing the lady in question a funny poem – which made her laugh – but even so, you don't need that kind of agro.

The second group of people are more of a nuisance. These folks assume that you've been looking at their profile because you were drawn to it by some irresistible force of sexual attraction. If you *don't* follow your visit with a gushing message inviting them into your life they can become impatient. Even abusive. I've had angry messages along the lines of "why look at my profile and then not send a message? Are you an idiot or somfing?" No poem was going to get me out of that one.

You don't need that kind of agro either.

But wait, what about that ability to see who's been looking at us, reading our profile – surely that's worth keeping? Right? That could be useful?

Not even remotely.

That 'recent visitors' list is the fast track to insanity. No good can ever come of it. If there's nobody on it (unlikely) you'll feel dejected and left on the shelf, but if there *are* people on it (more likely) you'll only start to torture yourself with this question:

"Why didn't this person contact me?"

With every new visitor you'll merely ask that question again and again, louder and louder, until one day you'll see the profile of someone you recognise – someone that you've actually messaged, but heard nothing from – and on that day that question will be a deafening roar inside your head.

And that, my friend, is agro you most definitely do not need.

Select the 'anonymous browsing' option.

Now.

Searching and Browsing

So, now that we've safeguarded you against dimwits and potential insanity, let's get back to browsing.

There are, broadly speaking, two methods.

The first is to look at the profiles that your site 'recommends'. You'll find them on your home page, on a side bar, along the top, in daily or weekly emails, or a combination of all these things. Whether there's any intelligence at work behind these recommendations will once again depend on the site.

An alternative approach is to perform a 'search'.

All online dating websites allow you to search their pool of members, and filter the results using criteria entered under 'basic information'. So a typical search might be:-

- Women who like men
- Within fifty miles of my location
- Between 30 and 59
- With photos

If you're *really* lucky you might be able to refine the search by specifying how long since they last logged on (an extremely useful option – and possibly the only useful option aside from sexual preference).

Let me put in a plea to keep your desired age range, earnings and education settings as broad as possible. Those things are far less important than you think they are. As we discussed at the start of the book, those things may affect how you feel about someone initially, most of them won't mean a thing within thirty minutes to a couple of days of your first meeting.

By the way, here's a top browsing tip: If you're looking at a page on the dating site, and there are links to several profiles that you'd like to look at (e.g. your search results), holding down the control / command key as you click the link will *usually* open that profile in a new tab. In this way you can open several profiles at once and work your way through them, rather than having to go forwards and back, forwards and back, over and over. Try it.

Personally, I gave up performing searches many years ago. I preferred instead to take a quick look at the daily profile recommendations that arrived in my email inbox. But *how* you browse profiles is actually irrelevant. The only really important thing is that you do, on a fairly regular basis, and when you do that you follow the guidelines later in this book.

Right after we've taken some action, of course.

STOP! ACTION POINT!

Master the Browsing Basics

Check to see if your site offers you a list of recent profile visitors. If it does find the option to switch it off and/or browse anonymously.

Start browsing profiles on a regular basis. It doesn't matter how you come across the profiles, it only matters that you do.

The Browsing Basics… on *Tinder*

When you start up the *Tinder* app, after a moment or two of communicating with the internet, *Tinder* will present you with the first of today's pictures. The temptation is to immediately start swiping; swipe that picture left (if it's not rattling your chain) or right / up (if you feel a stirring deep in your soul) – but do yourself a favour and hold fire for just two minutes. Tap the icon in the top left hand corner – the one that looks like a bit like a silhouetted head – don't worry, Mr or Ms Gorgeous will still be here when you get back, promise.

Tapping the 'head' takes you to your profile panel. It's here that you can select options to view your profile, edit your profile, and adjust some of the settings. What I'd like you to do is tap SETTINGS and scroll down to *'Discovery Settings'*.

Under Discovery Settings you have (at the time of writing[18]) four broad options; whether or not you'd like people to discover your profile, how far away you'd like your potential matches to be, their age range and gender. Now, how you set these is entirely up to you but it's worth bearing the following in mind:

Firstly, distance is calculated using your *actual* location, right now, and the location of other people using the app. This is extremely clever, *but not necessarily useful.*

As I sit here now I can look out of the window and there, across a large expanse of water called The Thames Estuary, is Kent. It's only twenty mile away as the crow flies, but because I'm not a crow, and I don't own a boat, it would take about two hours to reach by car. More than once *Tinder* matched me with an otherwise lovely looking Kent lady who was just too far away to make dating a serious possibility. Sure, *Tinder* will tell you how close someone is (when you tap on their main photo to view their full profile), but what it *won't*

---

[18] March 2018

tell you is what direction those kilometres are in – and that could make a huge difference.

There are other reasons too why you might not want to limit your searching to people within a given radius of your phone, which is why *Tinder* will let you *change* your location, at will... if you upgrade to *Tinder Plus*, which is basically the normal *Tinder* app without restrictions – after you've parted with some hard earned cash.

Let's take a look at that age range slider. You already know from an earlier chapter that I have strong views on how pertinent age is to a successful romance, and when it comes to *Tinder*, those views aren't just set in stone, they're carved out of diamond, and here's why:

Tinder pulls your age in from your *Facebook* profile. However, it turns out that whilst people are usually quite accurate about the day and month they were born on (presumably so that they can be inundated with online birthday wishes), when it comes to their actual *year* of birth – not so much. I've found forty year olds that *Tinder* says are twenty, and twenty year olds that *Tinder* swears blind are drawing their pensions. My advice is, as ever, keep that age range as broad as possible.

Once you've adjusted your Discovery Settings, tap DONE (top right hand corner) and you're returned to the Profile Panel.

Now you *could* tap that flame icon in the top right hand corner and return to the main screen – but whilst we're here let's make sure we're familiar with two other options.

Firstly, tapping your picture will allow you to see your *Tinder* profile as the rest of the world sees it. Have a quick look, just to make sure you're happy with everything.

If there's anything that strikes you as odd (such as the absence of your ABOUT ME text), tap the EDIT INFO button and you'll be able to edit the text, delete or add photos, as well as connect your *Instagram* account (should you want complete strangers to view that).

STOP! ACTION POINT!

Master the Browsing Basics on Tinder

- Set your discovery preferences
- Remember that 'distance' is as the crow flies and doesn't take into account borders, mountain ranges, or rivers.
- Remember that peoples ages are determined by *Facebook* and might not be accurate – keep your age range broad.

REVIEWING PROFILES

Whether you sit yourself down for an intense Sunday afternoon session of paging through search results from the ever more ingenious search-criteria you've devised, or whether you prefer to dip-in-daily to take a quick look at your 'matches' is completely down to you. But whatever you decide, I strongly recommend creating a process similar to the one we're going to discuss over the following pages.

In many ways, working through profiles is a little like being a police detective; it's a case of eliminating people from your enquiries, and adding the remainder to your 'list of suspects'.

This might seem a little counter intuitive, or negative, but whilst it can be a heartbreaking process – dismissing what initially seemed like such a promising profile, particularly if your inbox is usually more empty than not – in reality you're saving yourself from frustration and potential heartbreak further down the line.

So, grab your imaginary detective badge and warrant card and let's narrow that list of people you'd like to interrogate further.

Important Note: Most of this chapter once again assumes that you're using a traditional dating website. Whilst some of the advice holds true for *Tinder*, there's a special section for *Tinder* users at the end.

Stage 1: Beware Inactive Profiles

You'll remember earlier in the book that I sited 'dormant' profiles as the number one reason why you might not get a reply to any message you send. I have no figures on this, but I estimate that on any given dating website, 80-90 per cent of the profiles have probably been abandoned – which sounds a little off putting until you realise that so long as you've picked a good website, there'll still be several thousand active profiles, the trick is identifying them amongst all the dead wood.

There's no sure-fire way of telling whether a profile is dormant but a pretty good indicator is to look at when the owner last logged in. Most dating sites will display this information somewhere, usually on the profile itself, and sometimes in the search results.

Anyone who's signed in during the last week or so is probably active, longer than a month or two and you're wasting your time.

This is, of course, extremely frustrating. You stumble across someone who ticks all the boxes… and then you notice that the last time they were online was Sept 2008! It's often tempting to send them a message anyway, but you might as well write anything you'd like to say on a piece of parchment, seal it in a bottle and throw it into the sea – you'll stand a far better chance of someone getting back to you.

You might wonder why dating sites don't perform some regular housekeeping and remove all this dead wood. Why don't they automatically delete any profile where the owner hasn't logged in for x weeks? But then, if they did, there would be significantly less profiles for you to browse. And they need you to believe that there's a multitude of good looking folks out there hungry for someone like you. Were they to purge the dormant profiles they'd be deleting reasons for you to sign up for a full membership and part with your hard earned cash. Like grocery stores, they want to keep their shelves stocked at all times. Unlike grocery stores, they'll leave out of date products on the shelves if they have to.

Free Members

Most membership sites (sites where you pay a monthly subscription) still allow visitors to create a 'free' profile without the need to shell out any cash. It's how they can claim that it's 'free to join'. However, 'free' members are restricted in their ability to send and reply to messages, so if you – *a full paid up member* – choose to contact a *free member* (which the site's creators are hoping you will) you're *unlikely to get a reply* unless the free member parts with some money. And how likely is that?

Do you really need to ask?

Regardless of how gorgeous a free member might appear, unless you're using a site where they have the unhindered ability to reply, treat free members like inactive profiles; ignore them.

Important Note: This advice assumes that your dating website of choice has given you the ability to see who's free and who isn't. Sites that don't display this information in the clear should probably be avoided.

Stage 2: Beware Profiles Without photos

People that don't have a photo on their dating profile are most definitely the exception, rather than the norm, and in my humble opinion you have to ask yourself *why?* Why, in this age of social media and technology, would someone *not* have a photo on their profile?

There are only a handful of reasons I can think of.

The first is that they don't want to be recognised by friends, family, colleagues or – *ahem* – their spouse!

The second is that they're hugely self-conscious about their appearance.

The third is that they've tried to delete their profile and removing pictures is as far as they've got.

Now it could be that you're like Jon (remember him?) – a person for whom physical appearance just isn't a factor. If that's true I take my hat off to you – the world would probably be a better place if more people thought as you do. I'll confess that a part of me wants to warn you about the dangers of scammers, and how a picture would help you flush them out, but the truth is scammers know better than anyone that a profile without photos is going to be largely ignored. So that photo-less profile you've found is probably completely genuine. Better than that, your message will be one of only a handful of genuine messages that they're ever likely to get. So go ahead – read their profile, check to see when they were last active, and if you still like the cut of their jib send them a message.

But what if, like me, you happen to believe that appearances *are* important. And you've stumbled on an otherwise charming photo-less profile? What should you do?

It might be tempting to shoot them a message along the lines of "have you got a photo?" – some people actually state on their profile that they'll send you their photo on request. Let's examine how that scenario is likely to play out:

You ask for their photo, and what you receive in return is – how can I put this – a picture of someone who doesn't quite live up to the definition of 'gorgeous' that you had in mind. Now what?

I've made this mistake a couple of times.

You knew I was going to say that, didn't you.

The first time, the lady in question sent me a photo of herself sprawled near naked on a large bed – a strange choice of photograph to send someone you don't know. However, it did at least allow me to see the large tiger tattoo on her arm. I emailed back and told the lady in question that "lovely though she was", I am 'tatouazophobic' – I have a morbid fear of tattoos[19]. It's not true. I have no strong feelings towards body art or piercings of any description, but it was the only thing I could come up with to gracefully decline any further correspondence without causing upset. Did she believe me? I don't know. Was she upset? I don't know.

The second time (having completely failed to learn my lesson) I had no such escape route.

I considered telling this lady that I'd found someone else, but that would involve shutting down my profile which I didn't want to do.

I considered telling her the truth. I spent more time writing that email than I did this book and it still didn't sound right. I might be moderately good with words, but that email stretched my ability to breaking point.

In the end, I decided to simply not reply. Not long after, I received several fairly abusive emails. Clearly the lady was very upset. Perhaps understandably. But at least I'd learnt my lesson. From that moment on I decided to avoid photo-less profiles.

Let's digress for a moment and think about whether I could have handled that situation better, now that I'm older and wiser.

Perhaps honesty *would* have been a better policy. Pick my words carefully but make the point that in a world where it's simply not

---

[19] This actually exists. God bless Google.

possible for everyone to be attractive to everyone else, her particular dashing good looks just weren't blowing my skirt up.

Perhaps I should have thought "to hell with it – what does it matter if I cause offence? So there's a lonely soul sobbing their heart out over my brutally honest message. So what? Life's hard, baby. It's a dog eat dog world. Get over it." But that's really not me.

No, I'm afraid that if you have an ounce of humanity within you, if you dislike upsetting people, but you still place some importance on appearance, the only solution that works is to avoid getting into this situation, and make it a rule that you'll ignore profiles without a photo. Let's do that now.

DATING GOLDEN RULE #2:
IGNORE PROFILES WITHOUT PHOTOS.
THAT WAY LIES MADNESS.

But wait – what if they *are* drop dead gorgeous? By having this rule you'll never know that you've missed out on the opportunity of dating a 'hottie'!

Unlikely. Drop dead gorgeous people generally know that they're drop dead gorgeous. They nearly always upload photos (from the many that they have available). If anything, they have a tendency to skip the profile writing stage – in my somewhat extensive experience.

Yes but, what if they're a famous celebrity or something? Or maybe they're fed up with people who can't see past their beauty and want people to appreciate them for their scintillating personality? That could happen, surely?

Not as often as you'd like to think.

Okay, but maybe they don't know how to upload a photo to their profile. Not everyone's a tech genius.

That's possible. I've seen lots of photo-less profiles that say exactly that. But it really isn't that difficult, and sadly those people who struggle with the technology are also the same people who'll struggle to log back in and reply to any message you send them.

Okay, but maybe they just haven't got a digital camera, or a scanner, or a phone with a digital camera, or a friend with any of those things…

Look! One of the things you'll learn about online dating is that effectively you're looking for a needle in a haystack. Fortunately there are plenty of needles, and plenty of haystacks, but it's a 'needles and haystacks' game none the less and the only way to find those needles is to move on when you realise you're looking at hay.

Sites that blur photos

One of the more interesting challenges I've come across is this trend of blurring photos. Take for instance *Parship*. All photos appear fuzzy, and stay that way until you're:

- A paid up member of the site, *and*
- The member whose photos you're interested in has released them to you.

According to *Parship*'s website, they do this for safety and anonymity reasons, but it also means you have to engage the other person, at least on some level, before you get to see what they look like. Fortunately asking to see someone's photos is usually just a case of clicking a button. They get a pretty standard computer generated request along the lines of "Member X has requested to see your photos". Then they decide whether to grant it, also with the click of a button. It's all pretty quick, cold and emotionless. And therein is the closest thing we have to a solution: If looks are, to any degree, important to you, *before you initiate or respond to any messages,* click the button to send the 'reveal your photos' request – then forget about them and move on! If the other member reveals their photos (you should get a notification telling you so), great – send them a message, or reply to theirs, but until they do maintain 'radio silence'.

Stage 3: Beware The Scammers

Scammers are those members of the site or app you're using, whose ultimate 'end game' is something *other* than 'dating' – regardless of how broad your definition of dating might be.

For instance, there are the prostitutes. Their pictures are genuine, and they're more than happy to meet you for a date – but though they won't describe or perhaps even consider it prostitution, at some point there will be discussion of a 'fee'.

Another common scammer is the 'cam girl' – an online 'stripper' who'll happily exchange a few chatty messages but eventually try and persuade you to visit a different website, and pay money to watch her take her clothes off.

Then there are the stunningly beautiful individuals whose sole aim is to get you to visit or sign up to an alternative (dating) site, because they're "not on this site very often". Best case scenario it's just an attempt to lure members to a new dating site that needs members, worst case scenario it's a sophisticated way to obtain your email address, credit card number, and/or other personal information.

Finally, there are the more traditional scam artists. Those whose sole aim is to part you from your money. There's the charming widower / soldier posted overseas, who's either stuck in another country and needs money to get home, or needs a loan for another legitimate sounding reason. There's the beautiful young girl whose evil landlord will throw her out onto the street unless she comes up with the rent arrears. There's the lady or gent whose mother/daughter is very ill, or dying, and wants to visit them one last time, or pay for an operation to save their life. And then there's the so-called skint person who just needs the bus fare or petrol money to come and meet you! These are just a few out of the millions of sob stories being invented everyday by a scammer near you.

How can you spot these people?

In my experience, the most effective way is to simply check their photos (see next section). If you've been contacted by a prostitute, a cam girl, or an old fashioned con-man or con-woman, you can usually flush them out by merely seeing where else their profile pictures appear on the internet.

A prostitute might have their photos on an escort site, a cam girl will probably have her pictures on a cam-girl site, and your regular scam artist has probably stolen his or her pictures from some handsome dude's *Facebook* page, a porn-star's website, or even a minor celebrity – and you can find all of this out in the time it's taken you to read that last paragraph.

In addition to the suspicious use of photos, and the behaviours outlined above, other indicators of potentially scam-like activities include the following:

- Broken English, and poor punctuation in their profile or messages. Here's an extreme example:

> "I rather nice girl,am 18 years. At me green eyes,,light hair.My growth of 170 centimeters. Will be waiting for your reply or through an offline with my yahoo i.d."

- Frequent mentions of God in their profile. Scammers are surprisingly religious.
- A message that fails to comment on anything you wrote and could have been sent to anyone.
- Messages that start with 'Sweetie' or 'My dear' or something equally sickly sweet or inappropriate for an opening message.
- Profiles that state they're a model/soldier – presumably to justify the array of stunning photos.

Now clearly, not all models or soldiers are scam artists. Not all god-fearing folks are intent on separating you from your hard earned wedge. Let's not start 'flagging' the profiles of anyone who falls into these categories. And whilst we're on the subject, it's worth mentioning that just because someone *isn't* looking for the same kind of dating situation as yourself (perhaps they're looking for an affair, or multiple partners, or a sugar daddy) that doesn't make them a scammer either. The 'flag' button *isn't* for those people you don't like the look of, or whose life-style choice doesn't match yours, there's usually a 'hide' button for that.

What *does* make someone a scammer is the element of deception, coupled with an attempt to extract personal information or money from you.

So what should you do if you suspect you're being scammed? Four things:

Anti Scammer Step One: Stop communicating

Cease all communication. Immediately. No messages along the lines of "I've sussed you out you scammer scum" (I've actually seen that) – such messages only tip off the scammer. If they're smart they'll create a new profile and refine their scam before the website can do anything about them. Instead, it's better to leave them waiting for your reply whilst the website shuts down their account and warns others that they've contacted – and there will be others.

Likewise, don't start posting warnings on your profile no matter how bitter and let down you feel – it's a pointless waste of time, and it really doesn't look attractive to potential suitors.

Anti Scammer Step Two: flag the messages.

Seconds after making the decision to cease communication you should flag the profile, and any message exchange that led you to conclude you were in the presence of an arch-scammer. This will of course be impossible if you're no longer communicating through the site, so from here on follow this rule:

DATING GOLDEN RULE #3:
NOBODY GETS YOUR (PRIMARY) EMAIL ADDRESS,
FACEBOOK DETAILS, PHONE NUMBER, SURNAME,
OR ANYTHING ELSE
UNTIL YOU'VE MET THEM IN REAL LIFE.

The dating site can't take any action unless you can give them proof, and the best proof you can give them is a message exchange *inside* their site.

Third step:

Anti Scammer Step Three: Block 'em.

Blocking a profile prevents the owner of that profile from contacting you again. It usually 'hides' the profile too so that you'll never see it again. On some sites it even makes you invisible to them.

And finally:

Anti Scammer Step Four: Move On.

This final step – move on – is often the hardest part of this process, but move on you must. Erase the experience from your memory. Chalk it up to experience.

Scams change all the time – if you come across any that I haven't mentioned feel free to post a comment on the website[20], meanwhile, let's take my own advice, and move on.

---

[20] *HowToStopWaitingAndStartDating.com* – you could have guessed that really.

Checking Photos

Back in the early days of the internet, before it was even called the internet, web pages were just words. Nothing more. Now we live in a world where people are used to having their mug shot plastered all over *Facebook* and the countless other social media sites. And regardless of what you may think, when it comes to online dating that is a very, very good thing. The old saying about 'the camera never lies' might actually be truer than we thought.

Let's assume that you've received a message from someone you like the look of, or you've stumbled across a profile whilst browsing, and your heart is all of a flutter. Before you reply to or initiate any messages I recommend 'checking' the authenticity of their profile photos. It's quick, easy, legal, very revealing, and in this world of scammers, spammers and fraudsters, just good sense.

Whilst using your PC or Mac, right-click the image you want to check and select 'Search *Google* for this image'.

This is called a "reverse image search". As of this moment[21], this really only works on a desktop computers, such as a PC or Mac – it might not work on your tablet or smart phone, but give it another year or so and you'll probably be able to do this on every internet enabled device with just one click!

If you've done the above correctly *Google* will, after a second or two, return your search results.

Quite often, *Google* will tell you that the image can't be found anywhere on the internet – which is pretty odd as that's where you found it! What this actually means, in the context of what we're trying to find out, is that the image only appears on the user's profile but hasn't been there long enough for *Google* to catalogue it. By and

---

[21] March 2018

large this is a good thing. It doesn't mean that the image is *definitely* the user, but it's a strong possibility.

Occasionally, you *will* find the image elsewhere: *Google* will first tell you how big the image you gave it was, and links to where you can find other sizes. It might try and guess the 'name' of the image, as well as offer you an array of what it considers 'similar images'. More importantly, though, it'll list all the other websites where this image can be found.

For instance, were you to perform a reverse image search using my author photo you'd most likely find my *Facebook* profile, my *LinkedIn* account, my picture on my agent's website, my blogs, blog posts I've written for others, my author profile at my publisher's site, my author page on Amazon, and perhaps a couple of newspaper or magazine features.

A typical reverse image search might find other dating profiles (people often sign up for more than one site, especially if the sites they're on are free). Have a quick look at whatever *Google* offers you. After all, here's an opportunity to find out a little more about the person you're interested in, and remember; none of the information you're looking at is 'private' – you could have stumbled across it yourself given enough time on the internet.

That said, the only thing you should do is 'look'. Just look. That's all. DO NOT try and 'friend' them, do not send them a message on every site they're on – in fact, don't even mention that you've found their other profiles! Not now, and possibly not ever. That kind of activity will make you look like a stalker.

Back to those search results: Multiple matches from the same website you started on (such as *OKCupid*.com) usually means that a thumbnail of the image you're searching for appears on several profiles under a heading such as "similar users" – but it's worth checking. What would be cause for concern are numerous matches to multiple *Facebook* accounts in different names, multiple dating profiles where the user claims to live in a different country on each, and/or links to porn sites. When this happens it's reasonably safe to assume that the lovely person in the picture you're checking is unlikely to be the owner of the profile.

It's hard to put into words how bitterly disappointing this can be. If you're like me, you'll probably spend a desperate few minutes trying to find evidence to the contrary before accepting the truth: the owner of the profile you've found is attempting to pass off stolen images as their own.

Why might this be? There are four reasons I can think of:

The user doesn't consider themselves photogenic, or for some inexplicable reasons they haven't any digital pictures of themselves, so they've stolen pictures of someone who might look a bit similar – maybe – as a short term solution. Either way, they're probably hoping that they can talk you round when they meet you in real life, and that you won't be too upset.

The user doesn't actually expect you to believe that these are genuine pictures. They're just here to catch your eye – and catch your eye they did!

It's a joke profile. Those pictures that look a little like George Clooney, actually *are* George Clooney. And some bright spark thought it would be hilarious to create a profile using his images. George Clooney on a dating website! Oh stop, you're cracking me up…

The user hopes you'll believe these are genuine pictures, just as they hope you're the kind of person who might part with money, your email address, or other personal details. In other words, they're a scam artist.

None of these reasons, in my humble opinion, justify the means. At best it's misleading, at worst it's deception. My advice to you would be to 'flag' the original picture as stolen.

Having flagged the picture, 'block' the account and move on.

Now I'll admit that all this 'reverse image searching' can feel a tad intrusive. Right now[22] most people are completely unaware that sort of search is even possible. Whenever I mentioned it to friends the colour usually drains from their face. Occasionally, they rush off to

---

[22] March 2018

see if they have anything online that may incriminate them in some way. If you're feeling equally worried, now would be a good time to audit any social media sites you belong to, review the privacy options, and maybe purge a few of the more risqué pictures.

Plenty of people believe this reverse image search functionality is a bad thing. But then, plenty of people used to think that *Facebook* was a bad thing, heck – a few years back 'the internet' was a hard sell to some people. Some are still convinced it is a despicable seething hell hole of depravity. Whether it is or isn't is actually irrelevant. The genie's out of the bottle. There's no un-inventing it. And, regardless of your feelings on the subject, it's only a matter of time before this kind of reverse image search is common place. Until then, I encourage you to use this awesome technology for your own protection, and to increase your odds of successful dating.

STOP! ACTION POINT!

Performing a Reverse Image Search

- No results is a good thing.

- Results including one *Facebook* profile, *LinkedIn*, *Twitter*, other dating sites is also okay. And an opportunity to find out more.

- Pages and pages of search results including multiple *Facebook* accounts, links to porn sites, multiple dating profiles, in many different countries, is most definitely a bad thing. Flag photo as stolen. Move on.

Stage 4: Beware Misleading photos

So, let's pretend for a moment that you have a profile in front of you right now, and that the person you're looking at is a vision of loveliness. A god amongst gods, or a goddess amongst goddesses.

You have, of course, used *Google* to check their images and you're reasonably certain that the images haven't been stolen. Nothing else on the profile leads you to suspect you have a scammer on your hands. Can we assume then, that this is what they look like? Mmmm, maybe.

There are three things to ask yourself when looking at people's profile photos:

- How old is this photo?
- How much of the person can you actually see?
- Which is the least flattering photo on this profile?

It is, of course, very difficult to tell when a photo was actually taken, and although digital images these days have this information embedded in them, those aren't the images you should be worried about – it's the ones that were taken long before digital photography even existed that you want to flush out. The ones that are ten or twenty years old.

When looking at photos pay close attention to the style of any clothes you can see. You might not be dealing with a dedicated follower of fashion, but if the people in the background are wearing brown corduroy suits and thick rimmed glasses this picture might not be that recent. Look for any telltale clues such as landmarks that may have changed, old mobile phones, old cameras, old cars or other ancient technology.

Keep your attention on the people and items in the picture. Don't be fooled by a photo that *appears* old (such as rounded corners, or strange bleached out colours) but is actually bang up to date. Many cameras and websites have effects and filters that can give a modern photo that authentic 1970's look.

Treat studio photos, arty photos, and close-up photos with a high degree of suspicion. Such photos can be impressive and convey a lot of mood, but in reality they're next to useless. That's not how they appear in real life.

What you ideally want to see is at least one, preferably more, well-lit, full-length 'holiday' photos, or something similar – something which in these days of *Facebook*-photo-tagging most people can usually lay their hands on pretty easily. A profile without these kinds of photos might as well have no photos at all, and we all know how I feel about photo-less profiles.

By and large, the more photos a person has on their profile, the more relaxed you can become. Particularly if they look the same in most of them.

This is probably as good a time as any to introduce you to the third inescapable law of dating:

DATING LAW #3:
A PERSONS LEAST FLATTERING PHOTO
IS NEARLY ALWAYS THE MOST RECENT,
AND WHAT THEY LOOK LIKE IN REAL LIFE

And with that in mind, let's use that valuable information in the next stage.

Stage 5: Rate The Profile!

Some dating websites, these days, give you the ability to rate someone's profile or pictures, just as you would a book on Amazon or audible.

There's something decidedly 'icky' about doing this. It's one thing to admit, to yourself, if not publically, that looks *are* important, it's quite another to start giving people ratings.

However, even if looks *aren't* important to you, depending on how your dating site works, rating pictures might actually be a useful function. Doing so usually does four important things:

It marks the profile so you'll know if you've looked at it before. A huge time saver.

It allows you to be able to find all the people you think are hot (there'll be link somewhere to all the people you've rated). Useful for when you're in the mood to send a few messages.

On some sites, if you've rated someone highly, and they do the same to you, the website will send you both an automated message informing you of the fact. This alone makes rating pictures worth the effort. Nobody likes to make the first move, even more so when that first move is so often met by a 'wall of silence', but in this case the first move has been made for you, and you already know that you find each other attractive. It's like being introduced to someone at a party by a trusted friend, or *Tinder* but without all the other *Tinder* awfulness

It gives useful information back to the site that they might use in future enhancements to match people. For instance, *OKCupid* have used members ratings in a number of interesting studies and made amendments to their site as a consequence.

Assuming a site is using a five-star rating system I rate as follows:

5 stars – drop dead gorgeous, every picture proves it.

4 stars – very attractive, almost every picture proves it.

3 stars – the jury's out. Rubbish, misleading or no pictures.

2 stars – probably not that attractive, but maybe these pictures are old or particularly unflattering.

1 star – definitely not my particular cup of tea or any other hot, tasty beverage.

Some people use the ratings system to rate the whole person – their pictures, their question answers, the whole package – rather than their physical attractiveness. If this works for you, go ahead.

If your site *doesn't* have a rating function, or it doesn't work in the way I've described, then see if there's a 'private note' function, a way of leaving yourself an aide memoire, just check that these are totally private and can't be seen by anyone but yourself.

Stage 6: Read The profile

Enough of pictures! Let's assume that you're happy the person is who they say they are and so far you like what you see. It's time to move on and do the thing that almost every woman, on every dating site on the planet, complains that men never do: *Read the profile.*

I strongly suspect that it isn't just us men that might be guilty of skim-reading profiles. The world we live in – especially the online world – is so fast paced, so visual, so 'in your face', so distracting, that we find it hard to concentrate on anything for longer than a second or two. I can see why a large percentage of folks would baulk at reading a profile that might be a couple of paragraphs in length.

Clearly, however, *that's not you.*

You're the sort of person who's happy to sit down and read a book, so a two-paragraph profile should be no problem at all. Which puts you ahead of the competition in a couple of ways.

Firstly, in a page or two you might be composing your first message. You'll find doing so significantly easier if you have something to comment on. But secondly, armed with our imaginary detective badge, we're still on the look out for any 'show stoppers' – reasons *not* to continue.

What these final 'show stoppers' may be will be down to you. I encourage you not to get hung up over little things like their love of collecting My Little Pony figurines, or their collection of Doctor Who annuals – those quirks can be tolerated, even appreciated (after some effort) – but if they reveal that they're big in the church, that they were once a man, or that they've been married three times but divorced only once, and those things bother you, then congratulations, you've just saved yourself from potential disappointment – time to move on.

One such show stopper (for me anyway) are the charming folks who put the words READ THE PROFILE in big red capital letters at the start of their self-summary. This is usually followed by a paragraph explaining how "sick to death" they are of messages from people who've ignored their extensive list of relationship requirements. These people are best avoided. They are casualties of the online dating process. The frustration of trying to find that special someone has finally pushed them over the edge and turned them into demented lost souls. I call them 'banshees'. It's completely up to you, of course, but in my experience there's no saving them. They're so blinded by their frustration that even if you take the time to carefully pick through their rant and make sure you do nothing to aggravate them further, more often than not you'll *still* manage to trigger a tirade of abuse, and another update to their profile. If you don't you can expect an interrogation experience similar to being tied to a chair and having a light shone in your eyes. So let's leave these folks to wallow.

In some cases, reading the profile might actually be a challenge. If you're new to the internet or social media you might not be familiar with some of the acronyms and abbreviations that more tech-savvy folk use without a second thought and are generally considered acceptable shorthand.

It's really best not to try and guess what some of these abbreviations mean. For instance, LOL[23] *doesn't* stand for 'Lots Of Love'. And whilst that's a mistake that's unlikely to cause anything more than mild confusion, I'm reasonably certain the acronyms NSA[24], FWB[25] and TS[26] would have many of you blocking a profile, whilst the rest of you won't be able to compose a message fast enough – assuming you know what those letters mean. To help you out there's an appendix of common TLAs (three letter acronyms) and other abbreviations at the back of this book.

By the way, though there are some crossovers, such abbreviations *aren't* txt spk (text speak). Txt spk came about in the early days of

---

[23] Laugh Out Loud.
[24] No Strings Attached.
[25] Friends With Benefits (benefits being 'sex').
[26] Transsexual.

text messaging and is a way to reduce the number of characters needed to send a message by dropping vowels, thus saving time and potentially money. *Some* people use text speak when there's no need, which is considered by the rest of us as immature and annoying. I'm just saying.

Stage 7: Beware of everything else

Your final 'check' before you start concocting a suitable reply, is everything else your current suspect has taken the time to complete.

For instance, some sites have additional questions, quizzes or questionnaires – it's worth looking through their answers. Other sites allow a degree of 'blogging' – you'll be amazed what people will write in a blog.

And, finally, there's the 'basic information'. As we discussed earlier, I personally believe it's best to ignore things like age, eye colour, hair colour, facial hair, whether or not they're a smoker, a drinker, a vegetarian – these things usually make very little difference to the overall quality of a relationship. Some of these details can change overnight – people start eating meat again, they shave off their hair, they start smoking more, they quit going out every night, they get a year older – and sometimes when this happens they forget, intentionally or otherwise, to update their profile.

Likewise, ignore, or treat with a healthy dose of suspicion, any details about where they live, how much they earn, and whether they have one doctorate or two. Location, money, and education are, I'll admit, important factors in any relationship – sometimes – but not as much as you'd think, and people tend to lie about these details. Especially if they've read this book.

Whilst we're talking about things to disregard, ignore *completely* the utterly misleading size descriptions. It's always struck me as odd that whilst many dating sites ask you to specify your height to the nearest centimetre, when it comes to your width they shy away from asking you to declare your circumference with the same level of accuracy. I've seen websites that ask men to specify penis length (seriously, I have) but NO site, so it seems, ever asks their female members to specify their dress size. Instead they offer a selection of politically correct descriptions such as "slim", "athletic", "average", "muscular", "a few extra pounds", "voluptuous", "cuddly" and other euphemisms.

The problem here, is that these terms are far too subjective. Given this list of terms I would describe myself as *average*, but with diet books selling like hot cakes (pun intended) and obesity in this country reaching epidemic proportions your "average" person is probably quite large. But would I describe myself as "slim"? I've known some very, very large people who would look me in the eyes and describe themselves as "a few extra pounds", and some stick-thin ladies who would describe themselves in the same way. As a writer I feel the urge to point out that "voluptuous" describes a certain body shape and isn't really anything to do with size at all, and what affectionate person wouldn't want to be described as cuddly?

Finally, do check their religion, and whether or not they have or want kids – if those things are important to you. But otherwise, if you've got to this stage, and you *haven't* found a reason *not* to message them, well…

Stage 8: Add Them To Favourites!

If a profile manages to make it through all the above checks it's time to add this person to your list of potentials.

Now you might think "why keep a list? Why not just send this person a message?" and if so I applaud your enthusiasm. Go ahead and do that if you're of a mind (though I strongly recommend reading the section called 'First Contact' before you hit 'send'), but if you're *not* in the mood for message writing, or you're short on time, hunt around for an 'add to favourites' button, or something similar.

A quick word of warning:

Back in the early days of online dating, your 'favourites list' was just that; a private list of profiles you liked the look of. These days however, adding someone to your favourites isn't as private as it used to be – quite a lot of sites inform the other party that they've been 'favourited'. It's easy to see why they do this and it could be a good thing. It *could* save you having to make the first move if the other party decides to message you first, though I wouldn't rely on it as an alternative to messaging. It is what it is; your favourites list. And when you have a spare half hour, and you've read the next chapter, we'll be back to work this list of suspects, first let's summarise what we've covered.

STOP! ACTION POINT!

Reviewing Profiles

- Check to see when they were last active.
- Skip profiles without pictures (unless you're Jon).
- Check for scammer-ish activities (reverse image search and scammer grammar in the profile).
- Check for misleading photos. Remember:

a) How old is this photo?

b) How much can you actually see?

c) Which is the least flattering photo on this profile?

Rate the profile / pictures:

5 stars – gorgeous, every picture proves it.

4 stars – attractive, most pictures prove it.

3 stars – rubbish, misleading or no pictures.

2 stars – probably not that attractive.

1 star – not my particular 'cup of tea'.

- Check the profile text.
- Check everything else (question answers, blog posts, basic information).
- Add to favourites (or not!).

Reviewing Profiles... on *Tinder*!

Here's some good news. If you've chosen to use *Tinder* rather than a regular dating site, then reviewing profiles not just easy, *it's almost fun* – an addictive world of swiping pictures left and right and up awaits you!

But before you cast this book to one-side and start ogling pictures, allow me to give you just a few pointers, ones that will help soften the blow when, inevitably, you discover that *Tinder* isn't quite as awesome as you no doubt currently think it is.

Reviewing Profiles

Having optimized your *Discovery Preferences*, you're ready to start looking at pics. Click that flame icon (if you haven't already) and you should find that Mr or Ms Gorgeous is presented to you once again.

By now you know what the drill is. Swipe *left* for NO WAY, *right* for YES WAY, and *up* for YES YES YES YES WAY (more on that in a moment). But in my experience, *swiping* in any direction is the fast track way to madness – it's *too easy!*

Before long you'll find yourself sucked into that swiping groove; left, left, left, left, left, left and Oh Bugger! *Arrrggghh*! I didn't mean to do that! Congratulations – you've just sent the man or woman of your dreams to *left swipe hell*.

Can you get them back?

No.

Well, okay, there are two ways:

The first is to upgrade to *Tinder Plus*. Now you can take back your miss-swipes to your heart's content.

The second way, which doesn't involve shelling out any cash, is to completely delete your account (under *App Settings*), and start again. Mr or Ms Gorgeous *should* be presented to you again at some point in the future. Should.

Having actually done that – more than once – I soon discovered that a much *better* alternative is to use *Tinder* in a manner which naturally reduces the chances of this heart-breaking accidental-left-swipe situation from ever happening. How?

Avoid swiping altogether.

When you're presented with someone, regardless of your initial reaction, get into the habit of *immediately tapping the i-button* (the lower case i, in a circular button, in the bottom right hand corner of the photo)

This brings up the user's <u>full</u> *Tinder* profile and from here you can see just how far away they are, and whether or not they've written a *Self Summary*. You can also slide through any other pictures available.

Take a moment to do all this and you'll be in a *far better* position to decide whether or not this person could be *the one*. If they could, tap the blue star (or the green heart, but more on that in a moment) – if they're not really doing it for you, there's a red X right next to it.

No more swiping!

No more accidental left swipes!

Incidentally, you might assume that Mr or Ms Gorgeous has been chosen for you based upon their location relative to yours and the settings we tinkered with a few pages back, but there's more to it than that. *Tinder* also uses your *Facebook* 'interests' (including pages you've liked), and '*Facebook* friends' that you might have in common.

Whilst we're on the subject of '*Facebook* friends', those folk are automatically excluded from your *Tinder* matches, thereby avoiding the awkwardness that arises from being matched with your current, but *soon-to-be*-ex, boy/girlfriend. However, it's an interesting moment when you're matched with someone who you could have absolutely sworn you were friends with on *Facebook*. I guess now you know why you haven't been seeing their updates in your news feed.

Be picky!

Generally speaking, when it comes to dating sites (and probably dating in general), women are far too picky, whilst men are rarely picky enough. And when it comes to *Tinder* this becomes even more apparent.

I've heard many a lady *complain* that as soon as she swipes a guy to right – *any guy!* – *Tinder* will immediately tell her she's been matched!

Now if this happened to me (whilst browsing ladies) I'd be delighted, but apparently it soon loses it's novelty, and many women start to assume, correctly[27], that the vast majority of men are sitting there of an evening swiping right on pretty much every single female they're presented with. Way to go fellas. You've just made life harder for yourselves and every other guy out there.

Tinder tried 'fixing' this problem in 2015 by introducing the *super-like* – a swipe upwards, or a quick tap of the blue star button.

A super-like, as the name suggests, is your way of saying 'I don't just like the look of you, I *reeeeaaalllyyy* like the look of you'. At the time of writing you can use just one super-like a day[28]. Though if you upgrade to the paid version, you get four more.

One advantage of the blue star button is that those people you've super-liked can see just how strongly you feel about them BEFORE they make up their mind up about you. And it's funny how someone can seem just that little bit more attractive when they're boosting your ego and you know what excellent taste they have.

But the *problem* with the super-like is that a *regular* match, where one or both of you hit the heart rather than the star, now seems a bit… well… regular! A bit bland. A bit normal. A bit like getting the consolation hippo key-ring at a fun fair rather than the giant pink cuddly teddy bear. And *nobody* wants to feel like a consolation hippo.

So here's how to make *Tinder* work for you: forget regular likes (the heart-button, the right-swipe) – from now on ONLY use super-likes. Sit yourself down, *carefully* review the profiles *Tinder* selects for

---

[27] The NY Times found men are 3x more likely to swipe right.
[28] Actually every 12 hours

you, and when you find today's special someone (having looked at *all* of their pictures, and read their profile), super-like them – then <u>close</u> the app, and come back tomorrow.

There is another good reason for being this level of picky:

As soon as *Tinder* matches you with someone, the message window opens and you're expected to dive straight in with your first message.

There are two common feelings that can happen at this stage – neither of them are good.

Firstly, sometimes you'll suddenly realise that although you liked the look of this person – enough to tap the heart or star icon – you don't like them *quite* enough to send a message, get into any kind of conversation, go on a date, or potentially spend the rest of your life with them.

Well let that be a lesson to you!

Never like or super-like anyone you wouldn't be prepared to send a message to right now. Sure, you enjoyed looking at their pictures – but there isn't a button for that. There's only the 'I'd like to go on a date with you' button, and the 'No, I'm not kidding, I really *really* would like to go on a date with you' button.

Fortunately for you, you can un-match someone (I'll let you figure out how – that can be your punishment) but bear in mind that they'll know exactly what's happened (because *Tinder* told them about the match too, remember). So feel the shame – then never ever let it happen again.

The second common feeling upon being matched with someone is that although you still think they're hot, you're just not in the messaging mood right now.

Writing messages is hard.

At least, it is compared to swiping and browsing, and sometimes we're just in a browsing mood, right? I mean, couldn't we just leave that person in our matches and message them later?

No.

If you match – STRIKE NOW!

Scientifically speaking, NOW really is the *only time* to send that opening message. The longer you wait, the less sincere you'll appear, and the less likely it'll be that you'll get any sort of reply, let alone a date. If you don't send a message now liking them was a complete and utter waste of time.

But surely those rules are just for men, right? I mean everyone knows that the man should make the first move, don't they? So as a lady, you can afford to keep swiping and wait until that fella contacts you, right?

Good luck with that. Let me know how it works out for you.

No – the harsh truth is that unless you're prepared to strike whilst the iron is red hot, and send a message the moment you match, there's little point in saving your matches for later.

Let's make that a rule.

DATING GOLDEN RULE #4:
NEVER USE THE *TINDER* APP UNLESS
YOU'RE PREPARED TO MESSAGE SOMEONE
RIGHT NOW!

Want to know what message you should be sending? Jump forward to the chapter entitled *First Contact*.

So kids, what have we learnt so far about *Tinder*?

STOP! ACTION POINT!

Reviewing Profiles... on Tinder

- Check those 'discovery settings'; loosen up the age parameter, but be careful with the distance.

- Don't swipe – tap the i-button to see all of the pictures and the summary text.

- Don't use the heart button. Only use 'super-like' – the star button.

- You have one super-like a day. Once you've used it put the app down, come back tomorrow.

- Don't use *Tinder* if you're not in a messaging mood. You're wasting your time.

- If you match – send a message NOW! Not sure what to write? Skip forward to the chapter on First Contact.

USING 'CLEVER' DATING SITES

Remember when we were picking your dating site we discussed those 'clever' dating websites? Sites that do a little more than hope you'll stumble across your soulmate as a result of browsing out-of-date photos and performing searches based on pointless criteria. These sites, allegedly, use psychological principals and computing power to 'match' you with other members – members with whom you might actually have something in common.

I'm quite fond of these 'clever' sites. Whilst they require more work and investment (in terms of time, rather than money) they allow you to do everything we've talked about in the previous chapters, but take it up a notch. Theoretically, these sites take the guesswork out of profile browsing. Any one you contact should be more likely to 'get you', and therefore more likely to respond. And any dates you arrange as a result should be far more likely to lead to a second, third and fourth date.

All that said, much like their less sophisticated counterparts, there seems to be a right way of using these sites, and about half a billion wrong ways. But fear not. You have me. And if you considered my advice earlier in the book and opted for one of the more advanced dating services, then this chapter is for you.

Answer The Questions, Dammit!

All three of the 'clever' websites we discussed earlier (*Parship*, *eHarmony*, and *OKCupid*) work by crunching information you provide when you answer a series of psychological questions. In many, many ways, these questions are far more important than what you put on your basic information or self-summary. The matching algorithms can *only* work if you give these sites something to work with. With this in mind you should answer plenty of questions.

How many's plenty? In the case of *OKCupid*, somewhere between 100 questions (at the very least), and that point just before you're beginning to lose the will to live. You can answer questions whenever you like (it's not essential to do it in one sitting), and the more questions you answer the better – but be careful not to end up answering questions *instead of* answering messages or looking at profiles. Do both.

Now, this is important. Unless a question is mandatory you shouldn't necessarily answer *every* question that you're presented with. There are at least two situations where you should hit the SKIP button if there is one:

The first is if the question is really badly worded, such that there isn't a 'correct' answer you can choose. For instance, answering a question such as "would you prefer your first child to be male or female" – where the only possible answers are 'male' or 'female' – would be foolish if you've already decided that you don't want children, or if the *health* of your unborn infant is far more important than their gender.

Same goes for questions written by small minded people who assume all relationships are heterosexual, or monogamous. If you're gay or non-monogamous, skip such questions.

On some sites you can leave a note, further explaining the reason for your answer. Now you might think that qualifying your answer in some way would be a good thing. On the question of future unborn children you might say 'female' and then qualify it by saying "actually I don't want kids" in the comments field. Don't do this. The site's matching algorithm won't read your additional text, and instead you'll start being matched with all those folks who definitely want kids, and have a preference for girls. If there isn't an answer you like, SKIP that question.

Secondly, don't answer any questions where you wouldn't want your answer to count against you. For example, I once saw a question that asked which was the more heinous crime; book burning or flag burning. There really is no point in answering this question if you couldn't care less. There might be someone out there who you'd get along with famously, all other things considered, but they have a real thing against burning flags – but if in a moment of literary fondness you thought the burning of books was the greater of the two evils. Now the two of you will instantly be marked as enemies, and may never meet, and all because you answered a stupid question that you didn't really care about. (Excuse me, whilst I pause to throw another flag on the barbecue).

On some sites you can rate the importance of the question to you. So you might think, on the thorny subject of flag/book burning, that by marking that question as 'irrelevant' you've protected yourself against the above scenario. You haven't. It's not a big deal to you, but it *is* a big deal to the other person and you'll still be penalised for your book-burning answer. Skip it.

Telling the truth

More important than exercising your right *not* to answer questions is how accurate you should be with the answers you do give.

Unlike the 'basic information' – where you specify your age, location, earning potential, and education – when it comes to answers that are going to be used for matching it's *vitally* important to be 100 per cent honest.

Never choose an answer you *wish* was correct, if the more honest alternative is next to it. And never *ever* give a stupid answer to a question for comic effect. Both these strategies will work against you in the long run.

If you're really uncomfortable answering a question truthfully, look around for an option to keep your answer private, or skip it. Better to skip or hide your answer than to tell an untruth.

Go By The Numbers!

Imagine being able to walk into a room full of people and know, instantly, and without the need to say or do anything, who you might get along with, and who you should probably avoid – as if there's a light floating in the air above their head telling you this information.

That's what matching scores do. And once you've answered enough (good) questions, accurately, you'll suddenly find yourselves imbued with these super human powers.

This is a huge timesaver. Whereas, earlier in the book, I had you checking the photos and profiles of anyone who seemed promising, the compatibility score can save you time by allowing you to dismiss those people who – cute though they may be – you'll never get on with, no matter how much you lay on the charm, leaving you to move on to the next potential.

Note that the score doesn't negate the need for the usual background check, but now at least you're starting from a much better place.

Also, should you find yourself faced with several good prospects, all of whom logged on recently, the compatibility score gives you a way of sorting those people so you know who you should contact first.

And, it goes without saying that if you're going to use the search function on the site to find new profiles, make sure the score is part of your search criteria if you have the option.

You should take some time to familiarise yourself with how the compatibility score 'works'. Somewhere on the site you've chosen there'll be a link to a page, or pages, that tells you all about it. Read them. Make notes. If you can't find the level of information you're looking for use *Google*. Someone, somewhere, will have dismantled that score and described exactly what makes it tick.

By way of example, let's take a quick look at *OKCupid*'s scores:

The 'Match' score – this score is an indication of how many 'core values' (things that are important to you) you have in common. If you're looking for a partner you probably want this score to be in the eighties or nineties. Anything less than seventy per cent and you might struggle to find common ground.

The 'Enemy' Score – this score is pure gold! It's the score I trust more than any other. Think of it as a statistical representation of the fly in your ointment. It's like a crystal ball that allows you to see every argument you and the person you're looking at are ever likely to have. If this score is any higher than 10 per cent (yes, 10 per cent) you are in for a world of pain! Forget that person! Move along! Nothing to see here! Yes, they're cute – yes they written a witty profile summary – but go click on that tab marked "the two of us", select the option "unacceptable answers", and notice what an awful individual they are: They love cats! They don't want children! They burn flags! Run for the hills!! (Unless of course you don't want children, you love cats and you're easy on the whole flag burning thing... in which case you and I might get on fabulously...). IMPORTANT: as of now (March 2018) the *only* place to see the 'Enemy' score is when you're using the Browse Matches page, via a web-browser (not the app). *OKCupid* claim this because the 'Match' score (which you can see everywhere) already takes the 'Enemy' score into account – but in my experience the 'Enemy' score still brings something extra to the table. Use it if you can.

Beware Perfect Scores

Now that I've got you looking at compatibility scores it's only a matter of time before you come across someone with a fabulously high 'match' score.

Could it be you've found the perfect partner?

Unlikely.

Remember how I stressed the importance to answer a decent number of questions earlier? This is because compatibility scores are often derived by analysing answers to questions that you've *both* answered. An extremely high match score (or very low, perhaps even non-existent, enemy rating) is usually an indication that the other person has answered very few questions.

This is why it's still important to do your background checks, and why those checks should now include a look at how many questions they've answered, and why Golden Rule number five exists.

DATING GOLDEN RULE #5:
WHEN USING A COMPATIBILITY DATING SITE
SKIP ANYONE WHO HASN'T ANSWERED ENOUGH QUESTIONS

Believe me this is the toughest rule to follow, but seriously, forget them. Yes they're cute, yes they mention all sorts of funny/amazing things on their profile that you have in common, and the three questions they have answered all match yours... but given that you chose a 'matching' site over a regular dating site I'm guessing you've had enough of promising dates that turned out to be a waste of time. There are plenty of other cute people in the world – move onto the next profile.

Promising Scores.

So – you've stumbled across someone with a *reasonable* match score. You like their profile, and that picture of them holding those puppies is enough to melt your heart. Most importantly they've answered well over 100 questions. So what next?

As well as your usual background checks you should review their question answers to find out what you disagree on.

Assuming there isn't anything in their answers that raises eyebrows, the second step might be to see if you can fine tune those scores a little more. If you're able, take a look at all the questions that they've answered, but you *haven't*. Now, using what we learnt earlier, go answer as many of those questions as you can, and watch what happens to the score.

Let's take some action.

STOP! ACTION POINT!

Getting the most from 'matching' sites

Answer plenty of questions:

    - With brutal honesty – hiding answers if necessary.
    - Skip answers where hiding isn't an option.
    - Skip those where there isn't an answer that's 'correct'.
    - Or where giving an answer to a question you think is irrelevant might still disqualify you in someone else's eyes.

When browsing profiles…

    - Check the score before anything else.
    - Ignore anyone with a low match score.

Continue to do the usual background checks but…

    - Ignore anyone who hasn't answered enough questions.
    - Check their question answers for any show-stoppers.

Fine tune the score by answering any questions they've answered but you haven't.

Is It Worth The Extra Effort?

Some final thoughts on clever 'matching' sites.

In my experience, 'matching' sites are not as 'immediate' as their less-than-clever counterparts. What with all the questions and score checking it can feel like a lot of work. Tedious, and time consuming.

It can also seem like there are a lot less people to pick from, or that you're dismissing almost every profile (because of that damn compatibility score). But whilst this feels 'disheartening' it is, in fact, saving you from a great deal of potential heartbreak further down the line.

Imagine if, in the real world, all the people with whom you struggle to get on with were suddenly shunted sideways into their own universe. The traffic outside your window has vanished, and the sounds of the next door neighbours screaming at each other through the walls has come to an abrupt halt. For a second or two it might seem disconcerting – lonely even – until that certain someone from number thirty two cycles past on their bike, gives you a cheery wave, and that smile that always messes with your insides. At which point I'm sure you'll wonder whether perhaps the world wasn't getting just a little overcrowded, after all.

First Contact

By now your favourites list should be filling up with potentials. Any one of these lovely people could be 'the one', or 'the *next* one', or 'the one of *many*', depending on your personal preference. They are however, only *potentials*, and assuming that adding them to favourites didn't prompt a message, all the potential in the world isn't much use to us if that's how they stay. At some point you're going to have to make contact.

Like many online dating activities, sending messages isn't something that your average person enjoys. In fact, even though most people shy away from writing their profile, sending messages seems even harder to get right, and has the potential to be far more soul destroying. Before we get into the dos and don'ts, let me regale you with a torrid tale of online dating heartbreak.

The Tale of Tabatha

I once had a very lonely friend – let's call her Tabatha – who decided to give online dating a try. She found a website that appealed to her and would spend one evening a week scouring the profiles of other members to find that special person. When, in the early hours of the morning, she'd finally found someone, she'd carefully draft an opening message.

On the following page I've reproduced one of her messages as closely as possible, taking special care to change anything that might incriminate Tabatha or reveal her true identity.

"Hi."

Having sent this message she'd retire to bed and lay awake all night in nervous anticipation of the romance that awaited her. She'd get up at the crack of dawn to check her messages, then again after she'd showered and changed for work. Once at work, if anyone enquired how her dating exploits were going she'd probably enthuse about her possible new romance. By four p.m. she'd be itching to get home to check for the reply that by now must be waiting for her. There would be a slight moment of disappointment when she found her message inbox empty, and another an hour later when she checked again.

And again.

And again.

By the second day, desperation would set in. She'd find excuses in her mind as to why her future partner hadn't got around to replying (holiday, sickness, lousy internet connection), but one by one those excuses would wither and die until only one possibility remained.

They *hated* her.

Disappointment would turn to anger, anger to depression, depression to a night out down the pub with me. Whereupon I would sit and listen to the same tale I've just told you, only longer, and with much more venom and heartache.

There was only so much I could take. Eventually, like a spring wound too tight, I'd snap! I wouldn't be able to hold back any longer! I needed to *fix it*!

Much of the advice in this and previous chapters was honed during these pub sessions, but my advice, like the parable says, fell on stony ground. My approach required too much work. It was cold and calculating. Utterly unromantic. It wasn't how the world *should* work. And therein was the problem. Tabatha didn't want to live in *this* world, but some romantic universe of her own creation, where people meet easily, fall in love, and live happily ever after. If that world does exist, it isn't this one. This world, works somewhat differently.

Who To Message First

Much of Tabatha's pain and heartache was caused by sending messages, only to hear nothing in reply. Now clearly, Tabatha's brief messages left much to be desired, but it wasn't merely the brevity that was the problem. Tabatha could have significantly increased her chances of getting a reply – as can you – by giving a little more thought about *who* she should message.

If you're using *Tinder*, the job of figuring out who to message has been done for you. As soon as you match – I mean, the very moment the 'congratulations, you've matched' message appears – you need to write *something*, and that something needs to be good.

Jump forward to *Composing Your Message*, and get started.

For the rest of us using a regular dating website, there's a logical order which'll quickly determine where your time is best spent.

To begin with, work your message inbox *first*. If you have an email from someone you quite like the look of skip straight to the next chapter and send one back. Never mind that you have someone else in your favourites list for whom you would gladly give up one side of the bed and possibly a shelf or two in the bathroom. Statistically, you are *far* more likely to receive a reply from someone who's already initiated a message exchange, though those odds are dropping the longer you leave it.

Secondly, if you have any 'system generated introductions' – someone has added you to their favourites, or rated you highly – and again you quite like the look of them, check them out using the background check described earlier then use the rest of *this* chapter to compose a message. These people are also *far* more likely to respond to you.

Finally, when you've exhausted the first two possibilities take a look at your 'favourites'. Out of all of them, pick the one that was online most recently.

Now all of this seems incredibly logical, but when you come to apply it, the next inescapable law of dating will make itself apparent:

DATING LAW #4
THE MORE ATTRACTIVE A PERSON SEEMS, THE LESS LIKELY THEY ARE TO BE THE PERSON YOU SHOULD CONTACT NEXT.

Even if you're down to your favourites list and there are only two people on it, the least attractive of the two will *always* be the one who logged on the most recently. I'd like to be able to give you a psychological, scientific reason why this happens, but I can't. It's just the way of things. Murphy's law. The 'law of sod'. Call it what you will.

In this situation I use the more attractive person as a 'reward'. I allow myself to temporarily ignore my cold steely logic and send the hottie a message *but,* only *after* I've messaged the person who logic tells me to contact next.

Waves, Smiles, Flowers, Gifts And Other Virtual Nonsense

Having decided who we're going to message you might be tempted to use one of the inbuilt message 'alternatives' that so many websites have these days. Whether they call them virtual 'winks', 'flirts', 'pokes' or something else, they basically amount to the same thing; you press a button, and the other person gets an automated message telling them you did so.

Let's take a moment to consider what that looks like to the other person. You liked them so much that you took the time to move your mouse maybe half an inch, and click a button. Well gee. Good luck with that. Never mind that they were the only person who managed to make it through your extensive background check, never mind that you've narrowed them down from several dozen other suitors, they won't realise that – from their perspective you're probably tossing out winks and waves left, right and centre, which isn't the way to make someone feel special.

Let's make a new rule:

DATING GOLDEN RULE #6
NEVER, EVER, *EVER*
SEND A WINK, WAVE, KISS
OR ANY OTHER VIRTUAL GESTURE

Composing Your Message

Right then. It can't be avoided any longer. It's time to compose a message. Deep breath.

Oddly enough though, the *thought* of composing a message is usually far worse than the practice, and, like everything else, once you've sent a few messages they get easier and easier to do. More than that, follow the advice on the next few pages and I promise this'll be quick, and relatively painless.

What we're going to do here is compose a message of two or three sentences, no more. Whilst I'd love to tell you that short messages are more likely to get a response (they might – but I haven't any research to back that up) what they definitely do, is limit the emotional investment you're making. The longer the message, the more gutted you'll feel if you don't get anything back.

So, grab a piece of paper and a pen, and spend just a few minutes reading the profile of the person you'd like to message, and jotting down any and all of the following.

- What interests do you have in common?
- Have they asked any questions in their profile that you could answer?
- Have they said anything you could comment on?
- Is there anything in any of their photos you could ask about?

Once you have a couple of things, stop. Hit the message button, and leap right in. Skip the salutation, just start typing as if you've known this person all your life. Research[29] shows that messages starting with "hello" or "hi" or anything similar are statistically *less* likely to get a reply. It's the difference between standing at the bar and casually saying to the person next to you, "love your necklace" and

---

[29] Links to all the research used in this book can be found on the website at *www.HowToStopWaitingAndStartDating.com*

sticking out your hand and saying "Hello, my name's Peter Jones. I'm very pleased to meet you, and may I say what a charming piece of jewellery that is." One's formal and the other's a throw away line.

Of all the ideas you've jotted down, mentioning interests you have in common is statistically the best thing you can do. And pointing out that you noticed it in their profile increases your odds still further.

So a phrase like; "what a relief! I'm not the only veggie on here" not only highlights that you have something in common (plus points), but it shows that you've read their profile (more plus points).

You could also comment on something in their profile, and ask a follow up question. Or ask about something in their photos. ("Where was that taken? It looks like Rome.")

The important thing is to give them something to reply to – a reason to send you a message back. Don't go overboard – nothing too invasive – just give the other person an opportunity to open up and talk about themselves. So you might say:

"Ballroom dancing? Do you think you could teach me?" Or:

"Awesome views from that mountain top – where is that?"

Most people like talking about themselves to a lesser or greater degree. This is how you develop rapport.

Now, if you're a *Tinder* user there's a good chance that nothing I've just told you is particularly helpful. If you're looking at a *Tinder* profile with more than one picture or *anything* by way of a Self Summary you're extremely lucky. Most *Tinder* profiles give you nothing.

My advice is to start with one of the two things you probably *do* have in common; you liked each other, and you were relatively close when you matched. So you could go with:

"Fabulous! Really pleased we matched!" Or:

"*Tinder* reckons we're only 5km apart – do you live in Essex or were you just passing through?"

Compliments

General compliments about what people do, what they've written in their profile, or what they're doing in their photos work well:

"That's a great profile."

"I love your dog."

"What a cool job."

But note that we're complimenting things or activities, not the actual person. Dating gurus, scientists and statisticians all agree that it's a *really* bad idea to mention someone's physical appearance. Top of the list of 'things never to mention' are:

- How great they look.
- Any part of their anatomy.
- Anything sexual.

A few years back I used to moderate flagged items on my favourite dating website and it's astonishing just how many times I saw messages along those lines, and *always* it was messages from fellas to ladies.

I can understand, sort of, why expressing your appreciation of someone's loveliness might seem like a good idea, but this sort of direct 'flattery' really doesn't go down well. At least, not in your first message, or second, and certainly not in such 'graphic' terms. More often than not it backfires. So don't do it.

Forbidden topics

Though I dislike focusing on the negative there are a few other things you shouldn't do:

- Mentioning past or failed relationships.
- Talking about how lonely you've been.
- Making pointed remarks about how there seem to be nothing but idiots on dating sites.
- Cataloguing your dating disasters.
- Listing our hatred of dating, dating sites, people on dating sites, the way people use dating sites, or anything similar..

- Asking if they match up to your must-have criteria, and/or making threats if they fail to do so.

Does that list look familiar? It's pretty much the same list of things to avoid when writing your profile. To save me writing it out again later in the book, lets assume that these are taboo subject matters in every subsequent message, on your first date, the second date, and every date until your third wedding anniversary (and possibly not even then).

Write Proper

Finally, though it pains me to even mention it, scientists have discovered one other gem that everyone else has known for years. Txt spk, spelling mistakes, and lousy grammar, all hurt your chances of getting a reply. As many internet browsers, phones and tablets these days will actually check your spelling for you, there really is no excuse for poor communication skills.

Personally I'm not a huge fan of the *'emoticon'* either (beyond the good old fashioned smiley face). A row of tiny little party hats, followed by a dancing couple, a clock, a fire engine, and what might be a multi-coloured cat swallowing the remains of a mouse, usually fails to make me feel anything other than nauseous. Consider this; the last great civilisation to communicate via pictographs died out shortly after they finished building the pyramids. That can't be a coincidence. For the sake of your love life and the human species as a whole, I encourage you to use *words*.

I wish there was more I could say on the subject of composing messages. That I could offer you some sort of scientifically rubber stamped message-writing 'recipe' – a magic bullet if you like – that would guarantee the object of your affections will message you back, but… there isn't.

I toyed with the idea of including some example 'openers' that have worked for me or others, but the examples I have are pretty meaningless when taken out of context. Remember; it's your profile that actually does the work – your opening message is nothing more than a way of getting people to look at it.

Follow the guidelines above and you'll be able to write a message in three or four minutes, one that'll maximise your chances of getting to the next stage, whilst minimising the possibility of heartache.

Ready to click send?

Send And FORGET... on websites

Once you've sent your message, several things will happen.

Firstly the website will 'deliver' your message to its recipient, ready for when they next log in. If you're lucky the site will send them an email to prompt them. If you're *unlucky*, they – like me and thousands like us – may have switched that option off.

When they do get your message, unless you've been particularly dull or said something offensive, they won't be able to resist having a look at your profile. It's your profile – not your message – that you'll be judged on.

Then, if they like the look of you, if they've got the time, and if you started a conversation and made it easy for them to say something, *and* if there isn't someone else in their message box that they'd rather message – there's a chance you'll get a reply. Some day.

Not that any of this will matter to you because whilst all this activity, or lack of, is taking place you'll have done the following.

Firstly, if your website of choice has a 'notes' function (somewhere you can write private notes about a profile that no one else will ever see) you'll make a short note to yourself to say that you've sent a message. I usually type something like "message sent 29th October".

Next, you'll find that favourites button and *remove* them from your potentials. Yes, remove them. You've sent your message, there's nothing more you can do.

If you're feeling a little cavalier you might also want to hit the 'hide' button ('hide', *not* 'block') so that you never come across their profile again. At least not by chance. Don't worry, so long as you've hidden and not blocked them you'll still get any messages they send you.

Likewise, if the messaging system on the site has a 'sent items' box, empty it. You don't need a record of what you said – if they reply you'll get to see it again.

And finally, hardest of all but absolutely essential, you want to put them out of your head, and forget about them.

One of the most important online dating skills you can develop, is the ability to "send and forget". If you're doing *really well* then you should get about one reply to every ten messages you send. On average. Even if you're a woman. Even if you're a *younger* woman. Even if you're an *attractive* younger woman! But all those *non-replies* have the potential to claw at your soul and drive you crazy *unless* you can send and forget. And the only way I've found to forget, is to move on, and start the process again. Go back to browsing profiles, working your inbox and favourites list, and sending the next message.

For many of you this'll run counter to every instinct you have. It'll seem pessimistic ("why assume that I won't get a reply?"). It'll seem extreme ("is it really necessary to hide their profile?"). It may seem inefficient ("wouldn't it make more sense to at least wait for the outcome to the first message?"). It might even seem reckless and immoral ("but what if I get replies from more than one person?") We'll cover all of these objections in more depth in subsequent chapters, but for now let me remind you of Tabatha. To the best of my knowledge, she's still single.

Send And FORGET… on *Tinder*

Unfortunately, it's not possible to follow the 'send and forget' advice of the last couple of pages on *Tinder*.

On *Tinder*, once you've sent your message, it can be accessed by tapping the speech bubble icon (which appears in the top right hand corner of the screen when you're in swiping mode). The temptation is to keep checking back to see if you've got a reply yet, and believe me I know how frustrating it feels like when there's *still nothing there*.

Worse still, this frustration tends to grow and grow until at some point you start to consider whether you should send a follow up message.

Then perhaps another.

And another.

Anything just to get their bloody attention – after all, this is a person who said they *liked* you so WHY THE **** AREN'T THEY REPLYING!??!

Why people don't reply

This is one of the many failings of *Tinder* and judging by the feedback I've seen, pretty much the number one complaint people have about using the app; having been *matched* with someone they won't actually talk to you.

There are probably many reasons why this happens but I'm willing to bet that most times it's because of one the following:

Firstly, they did *like* you – but not enough to *date* you. Remember when you were back swiping and you accidentally 'liked' someone who was pretty hot, but seconds later when you were matched you realised you weren't that enamored with them after all? Now you know what it feels like.

The second reason, and the one I prefer to tell myself whenever I find myself in this situation, is that they *never* reply to anyone. They're just collecting 'likes'.

There used to be website called *hotornot.com*[30]. The purpose of this website was to find out whether you're hot… or not. You simply uploaded a picture, and then allowed other users of the site to like your pic, or give you a big thumbs down. I have no earthly idea why anyone would want to put themselves through this, but thousands of people did, every day, and presumably many people felt better knowing that x% of other *hotornot* users thought they were hot stuff.

For some people, *Tinder* is the new *hotornot.com*. Simply a way of finding out whether other folks find them attractive (and by other folks, we're talking about people that they themselves find attractive). For some, that's enough.

And I can see how that would be reassuring. In fact, I think there should be a 'use *Tinder* as hot-or-not' option right there under the *Tinder* preferences! Something that would allow those people to like each other to their hearts content, and leave us serious daters to get on and talk to each other.

Tinder?

Are you reading this?

Of course not. As I write this that option doesn't exist.

Resist checking your messages

So, until things change here's how to avoid the crazy-making hot-or-not folks on *Tinder*. Send your message. Then *forget* that you sent it. Don't keep dipping into your messages to check. There's no need anyway; *Tinder* will mark that little speech bubble icon with a red dot if there's something that deserves your attention. In the meantime go back to your once a day swiping sessions to find someone else you want to super-like.

Incidentally, in my experience people seem much more likely to talk to you if it's a super-like match, rather than a regular match. Another good reason to stick with the super-like.

---

[30] Actually there still is (Mar 2018). It's also a dating app that's suspiciously similar to *Tinder*.

Unmatching

After a couple of days, maybe a week, if you still haven't got a reply to your message and it's really beginning to niggle, you could *un-match* them.

To do this tap those three dots (in the top right hand corner of the screen whilst reading your message exchange) and select the *un-match* option. Un-matching will remove them from your list of matches, and you from theirs. You'll never see them again, and they won't be able to reply to the message you sent. But at least you've made your point; of all the people who think they're 'hot', you're no longer one of them.

The Ol' Cut & Paste

I really can't finish this chapter without giving a nod to that staple of male online dating strategies, *the ol' cut & paste.*

One of the clichés of dating is that whilst many women are far too picky (I've known women who write-off a potential suitor based on the *colour of his shoes.* Shoes, unlike personalities, can be changed), many men aren't nearly picky enough. Many men are basically looking for just one thing – someone who will acknowledge their existence!

These men sometimes find themselves in the situation of wanting to message every woman they can find. Pretty soon they discover the magic of cut 'n' paste. Put simply, a paragraph or two that can, with perhaps the odd tweak or two, be sent to anyone.

I used to do this.

For me it wasn't a numbers game – I still did my background check (all the stages that we've discussed), but it was a way of saving time when composing my initial message. And, in my defence, I'd like to say that my *cut and paste* text was absolutely superb having been honed over many years. It was cheeky, funny, self-deprecating, and ironically poked fun at people who send cut and paste messages! (No, you can't see it.) When it worked, it worked really, really well. But therein is the problem, because one day it stopped working.

I'm now firmly of the opinion that cut and paste messages have had their day. It's not uncommon to come across a profile from a lady who feels the need to put NO CUT 'N' PASTE MESSAGES on the bottom of her profile, and I strongly suspect that scammers (who nearly always adopt the cut and paste technique) are more than a little responsible for making people over sensitive.

The problem is that if a message even *looks* like it might be a 'cut and paste' its perceived value becomes no greater than Tabatha's one-word message, or the hideous virtual wink.

Worse still, if like me, you find it hard to use one word when there are at least ten amusing alternatives bouncing around inside your head, a long message (by which I mean two short paragraphs or more), however genuine and freshly scribed, could easily be mistaken as 'cut and paste'.

The lesson is clear.

Keep your messages *short*, *snappy*, and *unmistakably* written for the intended recipient.

Enough talk. Let's send a message.

STOP! ACTION POINT!

Making Contact

Figure out who to contact first:

a) Reply to any messages you've received (from people you like the look of, obviously).

b) Next; contact those folks who've rated you highly or added you to favourites (again, only those profiles that make your heart beat faster).

c) Finally; contact the most recently online person in your 'favourites' list.

Compose your message

a) Two or three sentences.

b) Comment on something in their profile.

c) Mention something that you have in common.

d) Send and Forget.

REPLYING TO MESSAGES

Everything we've done thus far – choosing a dating website, building our profile – has been for one purpose only: *to generate inbound messages*.

These messages, are your *leads*; people who, for the moment at least, like the look of you, and might, if you play your cards right, turn into dates.

If you play your cards right.

This chapter is all about those cards and how to play them.

Before we get into the cut and thrust of what to do, let's consider how you arrived at this chapter. I foresee three possibilities:

Possibility One

You're using *Tinder*.

Well of course you are.

In which case jump ahead to the section entitled 'Messages From People You Like'.

Possibility Two

You're using a dating website (or an app associated with a dating website). You've followed all my advice, built a fabulous profile, browsed other members on the site, identified the ones you liked the look of, checked those profiles thoroughly, and finally, sent a batch of short and snappy quips, at least one of which resulted in a reply!

Fabulous! You too should jump ahead a couple of pages to the section entitled 'Messages From People You Like'.

Possibility Three

You're using a dating website (or an app associated with a dating website). You've followed all my advice, built a fabulous profile, and *thirty seconds later* received your first message... which was, if we're being honest, a little creepy.

However, you did what I said and jumped to *this* chapter – which is a good thing too because this morning you woke to find you have an eye watering 72,546 unread messages! Most of which start *"Hey cutie/gorgeous/baby..."* or something similar, and most of which are very badly spelt. Some of those messages – the ones you've dared read – go on to ask if you'd be prepared to do something that you're reasonably certain is not only unhygienic, but in some of the more conservative states of America, possibly illegal!

And now you're sitting there wondering if this online dating lark was such a good idea. Right?

Relax.

Take a deep breath.

Believe it or not, this is all *normal*.

And I'm here to help.

You can do two things; either turn the page, and keep reading, or jump ahead to the section entitled 'Messages From People You Don't Like'.

Later, if you still find that there isn't a single message in your inbox that you like the look of, go *back* to the chapter entitled 'The Search Begins'. That'll sort you out. I promise.

But for now, let's deal with those messages you do have...

Messages From People You Like

So there you are, diligently logging into your online dating account, perhaps to do a little window shopping, and blow me down there's a little envelope icon that indicates you have a new message! You click on it, you read it, and before you get to the end your heart is beating like a drum as you realise that this, could be *it* – the day you've been waiting for! So what now? Should you fire back instructions on how to find your place? Clear your schedule for the rest of the week?

Not. So. Fast.

Whilst receiving messages is what we've been hoping for, before you leap in and declare your undying love there are a couple of quick things you should do first.

If their message is a 'reply'…

If the sender is *replying*, then so long as you've been working the site in the manner described in this book, you already know that this person has passed all your background checks – they're unlikely to be a scammer, there are no show stoppers lurking in their profile – it's someone you've already identified as a potential.

Still, there's no harm in having a quick re-read of that profile – just to see if they've updated anything, and another quick look at their photos.

Read and re-read their message carefully – it's surprising how often we miss something our sub-conscious doesn't want us to see. Did they say they were married (past tense), or that they *are* married? Did they say that they've "chosen to celebrate life", or that they've "chosen a celibate life"? Did they use a term or an abbreviation that you're not familiar with? TV doesn't always mean television. LOL doesn't mean Lots of Love. Polyamory has nothing to do with a love of parrots. You should probably *Google* anything you're not sure of.

But once you're done, if you're still happy, prepare to respond!

If their message came out of the blue...

If the message is 'unsolicited', well then, potentially that's even more exciting – this person liked you enough to make the first move! On the other hand it also means you have slightly more work to do, and that you should initiate a full background check.

Jump back to the chapter on reviewing profiles and do that now.

STOP! ACTION POINT!

If you receive a message...

If their message is a reply...

- Check their profile and photos for anything new.

If the message is unsolicited...

- Ignore messages from people without photos.
- Reverse image check the pictures.
- Check for scammer grammar.
- Check for misleading photos.
- Read the profile for show stoppers.
- Check question answers, blog posts etc.

Ping back a reply (see next section) if they pass the above checks and you want to.

Your First Reply

Replying to messages is a good deal easier than initiating them. By and large it's usually a case of answering any questions you may have been asked as well as tossing a few back.

As a general rule of thumb, it's good to keep your reply about the same length as theirs. If they write a couple of paragraphs, write a couple back. If they write a line or two, write a line or two back, and if they send you an annoying one or two word message such as "hi ya" or "you're cute" send back; "hey there!", "so are you" or "how's it going?"

It's a little like dancing, and for the purposes of this dance you want to let them take the lead – at least for a couple of messages. That said, regardless of what they do, keep the conversation light and breezy, and stay positive. It's fine to share a moan about the weather or how the site works, so long as you're not *really* moaning. Your primary aim here is to spark mutual attraction and develop rapport – nothing more! Leave the cross questioning and interrogation till much, much later (and maybe not even then). Likewise, stay well away from all the forbidden topics (mentioned in previous sections).

What should you mention then?

The important thing is to give them something to reply to – something to keep the conversation going. Too often I've had messages from ladies who answer my questions and nothing more. This makes them appear self-centred and dull, and leaves me struggling to know what to write in my next message. I'll be honest with you, many times I just haven't bothered.

Don't go overboard with your questions – nothing too invasive – just give the other person an opportunity to open up and talk about themselves. So you might say:

"Yep, that pic of me in the glider was taken earlier this year – have you ever done anything like that?" Or:

"Balloon modelling eh? What's the strangest thing you've been asked to make?"

Remember: Most people like talking about themselves to a lesser or greater degree. This is how you develop rapport.

Send and forget

Once you've answered their message, click send and then...

FORGET ABOUT IT!

Don't wait for a reply, just go back to your other messages and favourites list.

Believe me, this'll be even harder this time round. In your head, the voices will be telling you that there's someone, out there, interested in you and reading what you've written. You have the first sparks of a connection.

But they're just sparks.

And, without wanting to depress you too much, they *were* reading your messages and they *were* interested in you, but that might no longer be the case.

Do yourself and your sanity a HUGE favour – once you've hit send, delete the incoming message from your inbox *and* your mind. You've done everything you can – there's no point in worrying about the outcome, and thoughts along the lines of "maybe *this* is the one..." are dangerous.

Take it from me.

STOP! ACTION POINT!

Your first reply

- Match the length and tone of their message.
- Stay clear of the forbidden subjects.
- Give them something to reply to – a reason to message you back.
- Send.
- And forget!

Your *Second* Reply

Hello? What's this? *Another* message? Well get you! I'm impressed.

So what now?

Well clearly you should respond, and just as before you should keep it a similar length, avoid the forbidden topics, keep it light and fun, and concentrate on developing rapport. Do this right and you should get a third message without a great deal of effort.

No Action Point this time. You know the drill.

Reply Number Three

You're on a roll!

By message exchange number three or four you really need to be arranging to meet.

This is an important step. And here's why:

Beware the 'pleasant message exchange'

Not all dating pitfalls are unpleasant – some are downright *seductive,* which makes them even more terminal to your chances of long term success. One such pitfall, is the 'pleasant message exchange'.

It goes like this: You receive a message that makes you smile, laugh-out-loud or in some other way is just so darn cute. You reply and get something equally charming back. Before you know it you are pinging messages back and forth with this person who seems to know exactly how you feel about everything. Pretty soon you're logging on to the internet every few minutes to see if you have a new message, and as the days pass you find yourself telling this person things you've never told another living soul.

Eventually, sometimes weeks later, you arrange to meet in full knowledge that this is going to be the easiest, and best date of your life. It's not even a date really – you know each other that well – it's more of a formality. It would probably be simpler to meet at the registry office – or perhaps your bedroom – that's how close you are to this person.

Then you meet.

And disaster.

The first thing you notice is their voice. It isn't the deep, melodious, sultry lilt you were expecting. There are other things too. Perhaps they don't look like their pictures, or more accurately, the one you've had in your mind's eye – a culmination of the best two or three images from their profile and every daydream you've engaged in since. Perhaps they're not quite as quick witted as they seemed online, now that they don't have the luxury to think about their answers for a few minutes. And worst of all, perhaps they're looking at you in a way that suggests similar thoughts might be going through their head.

By now of course, you'll have realised that this has happened to me. More than once. And me being me I have a theory as to why this happens. It's a little like when you see a movie, having read the book. More often than not you're disappointed because the characters you had in your head when you read that story – their voices, how they looked, perhaps even what they wore or the setting they found themselves in – are different to what you now see on the screen. Well, of course they are. When you're reading, most of the character details come from *your* imagination. And as a result your Mr Darcy looks very different to the one that the casting director chose when they decided to turn the book into a film.

And that's what happens with online dating. *You fill in the gaps.* And the longer you correspond with people the more gaps you fill, until what you have in your head is a fully formed character who's charming, and beautiful, and intelligent, and witty, and more to the point, totally complimentary to yourself. The chances of that character being anything like the *real* person sending the messages you so love and enjoy are, sadly, slim to none. Worse still, the 'real person' is likely to fall short of your creation.

This is not the greatest of starts to any relationship. In my experience, it's usually the end.

For this reason, it's very important to get *off-line* and into the *real* world as soon as you can, before your imagination starts creating someone who doesn't exist.

Hmmmm. We haven't had a rule for a while.

DATING GOLDEN RULE #7
BY MESSAGE NUMBER 3 OR 4
YOU SHOULD BE
ARRANGING TO MEET.

There are a couple of reasons why people don't arrange to meet as quickly as they should.

One reason is most certainly because they're enjoying the messages, and there's a fear that once the dating starts the messages will end. That's a valid fear. It's also probably true. But let's just get this clear in our heads – those lovely charming messages have the power to kill any possibility of romance if you let them go on too long.

The second reason people hesitate to arrange a date is because it feels far too big a step. Messaging online is quick, easy, fun, flirty. Dating is scary, hard work, and (once you've factored in buying a new outfit, going to the hairdressers, and stressing about anything and everything) lasts about three days.

It's also hard to know where to suggest for a first date. The fact you're reading this book probably means you're old enough to consider a trip to the local 'cinema' a little juvenile. So your choices are what? A few drinks? A meal? A few drinks, then a meal, then more drinks?

Coffee.

'Meeting for coffee' is the antidote to all this 'first date' nonsense. For starters it doesn't even feel like a date. It's coffee. You'll barely be there long enough to take your coat off. More than that, you can meet for coffee mid-morning, in your lunch hour, mid-afternoon, after work, or early evening. It's definitely something that can be sandwiched between other appointments, in fact, there's a school of thought that says you should make sure it is, so that there's a clear start and (more importantly) *end* to the 'date'. Even if that second appointment is actually 'fictitious'.

Just so we're clear, when I say 'meet for coffee', I mean meeting for coffee, tea, hot chocolate, or any other non-alcoholic beverage – perhaps with the addition of a slice of cake – in a coffee shop, lasting somewhere between half an hour to an hour.

If 'coffee' goes well *then,* you can talk (later, online or over the phone) about having that scary first date. Except that it'll be a lot less scary. It might even be fun.

There's more I need to say on this, but for now your aim is to arrange 'coffee' as soon as you can.

Beware (Tinder) 'chat' mode

Similar to the 'pleasant message exchange' are those apps or websites where the conversation is less like email and more like a virtual-'chat' or text message exchange. You type your message, and ding – a second or two later back comes a reply. You respond, and ding, so do they.

Now this can be a lot of fun, particularly if you weren't actually trying to work, drive, eat, talk to someone else, watch TV, or anything else... but I've come to the conclusion it can quite easily turn into a *'pleasant message exchange'* – albeit masquerading as something else – and if you're not careful, this delightful bout of techno flirting might very easily become both the start, middle, and end, of your *entire* short-lived relationship.

So as soon as you find yourself firing short one-liners back and forth, you should jump right in and suggest that the two of you meet up, for coffee.

Avoid, if you can, exchanging phone numbers, or suggesting a phone conversation – not unless you're prepared to dial that number RIGHT NOW in order to secure that date.

Above all DON'T fall into the trap of suggesting you'll call or message them *later*. That rarely works. If *later* ever happens, you'll find the mood has changed. He or she won't seem the same some how. The magic will be lost. You just won't feel the same. And that date will never be arranged.

Right now is the golden moment: Arrange that coffee date.

STOP! ACTION POINT!

Third Reply

Don't fall into the trap of endlessly tossing back and forth flirty messages. Instead...

- Arrange to meet as soon as you can.
- For 'coffee'.
- If you find yourself in a virtual 'chat' situation, bring the conversation round to arranging coffee.
- Never fall into the trap of suggesting you'll call or message them later.

Messages From People You *Don't* Like

So there you are, diligently logging into your online dating account or app, perhaps to do a little window shopping, and blow me down there's an icon that indicates you have a new message! You click on it, you read it, and... oh... hmmmm.

Not every message you receive is going to be one you want to reply to. In fact sadly, most of them won't be. But just as we took our time to vet and respond to the messages we liked the look of, there's a similar strategy for those we want nothing more to do with – a strategy designed to keep us safe, and free from disillusionment and disappointment.

Beware the trolls

The internet has its fair share of weirdoes. I'm tempted to tell you there are no more of them online than there are in real life, but that doesn't seem to be the case. Whereas you can cross the road to avoid the bottle wielding madman on the other side, leaving him to shout at the pigeons, it isn't always as easy online.

One such internet weirdo is the 'troll'. Trolls are people who get a buzz out of insulting people online and causing the maximum amount of upset they can.

There seem to be two types of troll – those that seem perfectly pleasant to start with and build up their abuse over time (probably to see how long you'll put up with it), and those that launch straight into a hefty round of insults. Both share a common goal; to rile you and provoke a response. And the more you respond – particularly if your response is emotional – the more you're giving the troll what they crave.

You could, mistakenly, decide to treat these idiots to a dose of their own medicine, roll up your sleeves and give as good as you get. But trolls have no soul. To them you're merely raising the stakes. They'll see your insult about their questionable parentage and raise

174

you the possibility of multiple sexual encounters in public locations with poorly selected partners. Trolls feed on negativity.

You could decide to counter their negative energy with Zen-like calm. But to the troll you're now a challenge. And they'll keep at you, until they break you.

There is only one effective form of defence against a troll. Deny them the very thing they want: A response. Don't answer that message. Just delete it. And forget it.

There are two other forms of 'troll response' that are worth considering. Firstly, if the site gives you the ability to block, do so. It's one click. Secondly, if the site allows you to flag messages consider this option too. Chances are the site's moderators will boot the troll off the site.

Beware the 'Always Reply' Trap

It's not just trolls that hate to be ignored. One of the most disheartening things about online dating is receiving no response to a message you've invested time and effort into writing. Actually, never mind online dating, it's one of the more annoying things about any form of communication. An unanswered letter, an email that goes ignored, even a text message that fails to generate a reciprocal response – it can really irk!

Experience a few of these irkish incidents and you might become the sort of person who vows to respond to every genuine message, even if that response is to politely decline whatever's on offer. You might even put this promise in your profile somewhere, and come to the conclusion that the world would be a better place if everyone did the same.

It wouldn't.

Sometimes no response is better than the most crafted of carefully worded replies.

At some point you're going to receive a message from someone with whom you just don't click, and it may be for reasons that you can't quite put your finger on. And whilst, being a nice person, your gut reaction is to send back a politely worded message that talks about chemistry or the lack of, nine times out of ten that just won't work.

Were you to go down this road one of two possible outcomes awaits you. Firstly, the other person may take massive offence. They'll waste no time in telling you that, actually, they were doing you a favour by messaging you in the first place, but they see now that you're nothing more than a trumped up evil doer, and they hope you rot in hell for all eternity!

The second possibility is that the sender sees your reply as an opportunity to negotiate. They'll address any concerns you've raised in your message, and tell you that they *can* be the very person you're looking for – if you just give them a chance. In short, having got your attention they have no intention of letting it go. After an exchange of emails where your messages invariably start with the words, "I'm sorry, but…" you'll eventually be back to the first scenario, adding another name to the list of people who want to see you burn in the fires of Hades from now until the end of time.

Over the years, I've tried numerous 'letting people down gently' approaches, and I've come to the conclusion that there's no good way of doing it. Often I've searched for some practical reason why a relationship with the sender might be doomed – such as distance, or a very low match score, or my invented fear of tattoos – but more than once I've been told that they actually live a lot closer than the location on their profile, so that's not a problem, or I've been offered friendship instead – and suddenly I'm back to negotiating again.

The only answer I've found – harsh though it may seem – is to simply never reply in the first place.

Yes, I'm another person adding to the frustrations of many a disillusioned online dater, but given the alternatives, which seem to cause so much more upset, it's the best of a bad bunch.

Breaking off a message exchange

Which brings me on to the third type of unwanted message. The 'message exchange', which no longer looks as promising as it did at the outset.

It can happen. You receive an otherwise charming message, and after all the usual background checks, bat one back. You receive a second message, just as promising as the first, and so you send back another reply. But by message three or four (remember, you're supposed to be arranging coffee by this point) something's not quite right. You're not feeling 'it' any longer. You don't want to arrange coffee. Or anything else.

What do you do?

The first thing is to be honest. *With yourself.* Has replying to these messages become something of a chore? Are you continuing this message exchange merely because this is the first bite of interest you've had in a while? Do you – when you dig deep inside and examine your true feelings – want out? If the answer is yes, *you need to break off the exchange.*

Let's talk about that for a second because there will be those amongst you who will find this the hardest thing in the world. If you're a sensitive person, if you've been brought up to be a nice, polite individual, or if it's been a while since you had a relationship and you are, not to put too fine a point on it, a bit desperate – this will be extremely difficult. But, and I speak as someone who's made this mistake more than once, break it off you must, because life's too damn short and it'll be much, *much* harder later on.

You might think, as I used to, that you'll feel some excitement again when you actually meet. You won't. Though I dearly wish I had some science to back up my argument, my own experience is that the initial message exchange (before coffee) should *always* be fun and promising – if it isn't you should treat that as an early warning that a future relationship is impossible.

So how do you break off the exchange?

Your first and best option is to simply not reply. This is often easier than you'd think. Take a look at their last message: Have they asked a question? Is there anything about it which is inviting comment? If not there's a strong possibility that they are, in fact, feeling exactly the same as you. If their messages are fairly brief and taking a day or more to get to you, then all you need to do is delete their last message and that's the last you'll ever hear from them.

On the other hand, if their messages are longer, full of questions, come hot on the heels of any reply you may have sent – to put it another way, if they still seem keen – *not replying* might not cut it. Try it and see.

If 'not replying' fails to work – or it just doesn't appeal to you – a second option might be to come clean. If the person you're messaging is reasonable, and especially if your grounds for wanting out are practical (say 'distance' or 'kids' or 'incompatible lifestyles'), or you have a fundamental difference of opinion over key issues ('veganism', 'religion', 'politics' etc), you might be able to cobble together a polite message explaining why you don't see a romantic future. Briefly point out your differences if you must, but avoid debating them. Don't answer any questions they've asked – stick rigidly to the matter at hand. Keep your message friendly, but also keep it short. One paragraph. No more. Then finish it up with a genuine, heartfelt, line about how you "hope they'll meet someone nice". Notice we've completely failed to suggest they "stay in touch", or become "friends". That's intentional. Don't start offering 'consolation prizes' or 'glimmers of hope'.

If you've pulled off 'option two' you'll receive a similar response back, along the lines of "no worries, you too". Or you might receive no response at all. Either way, leave it there. No further messaging is necessary.

If, on the other hand, you failed to hit the mark, you'll almost certainly receive a tirade of abuse. Commiserations. You have my sympathy. But again, leave it there. <u>Don't</u> go sending apologies. <u>Don't</u> go making excuses. <u>Don't</u> justify yourself or answer any questions. And <u>don't</u> get into negotiation. You'll only dig yourself into a deeper hole and ultimately cause more pain. *Let them hate you*, whether you deserve it or not. Then delete the message, walk away, and chalk it up to experience.

Your last option is my least preferred. I call it 'souring the milk', and I recommend it only in extreme circumstances, when the previous two options don't seem possible. The idea is to make your messages shorter and shorter, answer questions but invite no further comment, and take longer to reply each time. Theoretically, this should make you less attractive, and – if you've done it right – there will come a point where no reply is necessary.

It must be said, though, this option feels cowardly, and more importantly, only works about half the time. The odds are that you're just as likely to get the same tirade of abuse that option two would have given you – which makes me wonder whether it wouldn't just be better to man up, and stick to the first two options.

But it's your choice.

Let's take some action.

STOP! ACTION POINT!

Replying to messages
(from someone you don't like)

- Ignore messages from Trolls. Do not respond. Consider blocking and flagging.

- Be discerning with who gets a response from you. Not replying is kinder in the long run.

- When breaking off a message exchange you have three options:

Option 1: you might be able to get away with <u>not</u> replying.

Option 2: if you're emailing a reasonable person, a short, honest message might be all you need.

Option 3: In the absence of options 1 and 2 consider 'souring the milk'.

'WORKING' THE DATING SITE / APP

Right. So... Let's have a recap of where you are:

You selected your photos. Chose your dating site. Or app. Wrote a self-summary. Signed up and created your profile. Learnt how to browse, search for other members, perform a background check, and create a list of potentials. Maybe you've even uncovered the mystery of the 'compatibility' score.

Either way, you're sending out messages, replying to others, and gently ignoring the odd one or two. You're spending maybe a couple of hours a week, total, in an online dating frenzy of messaging, browsing, and background searches.

Aren't you?

Exclusivity

In the US it's pretty much acceptable to be 'dating' more than one person at a time (where 'dating' *might* involve nothing more than dinner and a few drinks). Date someone for a while and you might then have a conversation about whether to go 'exclusive'.

Here in the UK however, there's an expectation that once you start dating someone you're *not* dating any one else – there's no 'are we exclusive?' conversation, the exclusivity has already started.

However, like Tabatha (earlier in the book), many of my (female) friends begin that period of exclusivity pretty much from their very first message. From the very moment they've found a profile they like the look of they only have eyes for that person. They send that first message and wait. They delete any others that arrive in the meantime. When they finally get a reply from their 'chosen one', they bat one back and continue to be steadfast and loyal. And all the time that emotional investment builds and builds until, like Tabatha, something 'goes wrong', and then… they're crestfallen.

Though, I don't have any research to back it up, I'd wager that the 'emotional investment' is part of the problem. Have you ever noticed how the more you want something the less likely it seems you'll get it?

Notice too, that the 'Tabatha' scenario only seems to happen to women. Generally speaking, young heterosexual men learn early on that the odds are stacked against them. For every girl they're interested in perusing there will be a dozen other guys fighting for the attentions of the same girl – many of them older, many of them with cars. After a while we come to the conclusion that successful dating is a 'numbers' game. It's why we sometimes favour the cut-and-paste approach to messaging. It doesn't mean we're any better at taking rejection, but it does mean that 'exclusivity' doesn't seem like such a great idea. At least in these early stages.

Therefore, I humbly introduce you to the next rule of online dating:

DATING GOLDEN RULE #8:
'DATING EXCLUSIVITY' IS ONLY FOR
PEOPLE YOU'VE DATED AT LEAST ONCE,
IN REAL LIFE
(AND EVEN THEN, ONLY IF YOU FEEL THE NEED)

Surely I'm not suggesting dating more than one person at a time?
    Possibly.

But I'm willing to bet that you're not in that position – *yet.* I'm betting any dates you've been offered have been few and far between, and that getting to the dating stage has been akin to climbing a slightly greased mountain in a strong wind. I'm here to tell you that it doesn't have to be that way. And to offer you a big bag of doughnuts.

The Doughnut Machine

Here in sunny Southend-on-Sea, along the south-east coast of England, we have a penchant for doughnuts. Take a walk along the sea-front and you'll eventually come to one of several kiosks selling fresh doughnuts – cooked to order.

The process takes only a few minutes and part of the fun is watching the antiquated doughnut machine at work: Firstly, blobs of doughnut mixture are dolloped into a tray of scalding hot oil, whilst a mini wave- machine ensures that the row of doughnuts-in-the-making float sedately towards a 'flipper'. The flipper flips the doughnuts over, into a second oil bath, and another wave-machine gently wafts them towards another flipper – which flips them out of the oil, and dumps them in sugar. Finally, a highly trained operative turns the doughnuts with a pair of tongs, sprinkles with cinnamon, and pops them into a paper bag.

It's a doughnut production line. And with the exception of the part where the operative hands you a bag full of scalding doughnuts for you to burn your fingers and the roof of your mouth on, it's similar – kind of – to my approach to dating. Potential dates are like dollops of doughnut mixture, and many many dollops have to pass through a number of stages before you finally, er, get your sticky mitts on just one of them.

Why *many*? Why not squirt a single dollop of doughnut mixture into the oil and waft it as quickly as possible through the oil, over the flipper, through the oil again, into the sugar, and finally into your bag? Because your dating 'doughnut machine' isn't in a kiosk. It's on a shipping trawler. In the middle of the ocean. In a force ten gale.

In these adverse conditions most of the doughnut mixture will never make it into the oil. Waves will come from all directions. Most doughnuts-to-be will get stuck on the side. Very few will make it to the first flipper. Fewer still will make it through the second batch of oil. Only occasionally will a lone doughnut make it as far as the sugar.

If you adopt the one-doughnut-at-a-time approach, you'll be waiting a very, very long time to get to the point where you can sprinkle some cinnamon on a hot sugary treat.

More than that, though, every failed doughnut will feel like a catastrophe. The frustration will build and build. And when the coastguard finally makes an appearance they'll find you sobbing in a corner, surrounded by bits of doughnut machine and an oily doughnut mix.

I don't want you to be that person. I want doughnuts for everyone. And the only way for that to happen, is to have several prospective dates each at the different stages of the dating process.

Della's Theory Of 'So-What'

Author Della Galton is a bit of a legend in the world of women's magazine fiction. Over the past 25 years she's had over 1000 short stories *published*. That's pretty much one a week. But anyone who knows anything about short fiction will tell you that it's not particularly easy to get published. The competition is stiff. The odds are stacked against you. And then there's the rejection.

I don't think Della will mind when I tell you that despite her popularity and success, those stories that make it into print might have been rejected, sometimes several times, by other magazines, before they eventually found a home.

I once asked Della how she managed to keep going in the face of all that rejection and she told me that it was due, in part, to her theory of 'so what?': At any given moment Della has *fifty* or so stories, sitting on the desks of fiction editors all over the world. Why so many? Because that's what it takes to generate a 'so what?' response when one of them gets rejected. When one story bites the bullet, forty nine are still left on the table.

Della's theory of 'so-what?' doesn't just work for magazine writing, it'll work for job interviews, sales work, soufflé baking – anything where you're emotionally invested in the outcome. And that includes dating.

Now, I realise all this talk of rejection, of strategies, of 'so what?', of dating doughnut machines – it must all seem a little cold and calculating. Like I've taken what should be a fun, exciting, and romantic process, and removed all those elements. Trust me. It's actually the reverse. There will be plenty of romance, fun, and excitement – but you won't need me to tell you what to do when those elements appear. I'm reasonably certain you'll have that completely covered. Which is why I'm concentrating on making sure you get to that point.

Now that we've established that, let's recap how an average session in front of your online dating doughnut machine should look.

STOP! ACTION POINT!

Working Your Dating Site

- Reply to messages from people you've been talking to. And remember: arrange to meet for coffee after the third message.

- Perform background checks and reply to messages from new people.

- Follow up on system introductions.

- Work your favourites list (your potentials).

- Browse for new profiles, perform background checks, add to favourites.

- Remember the eighth golden rule of online dating:

DATING GOLDEN RULE #8:
DON'T BE A TABATHA.
'DATING EXCLUSIVITY' IS FOR
PEOPLE YOU'VE DATED AT LEAST ONCE,
IN REAL LIFE
(AND EVEN THEN, ONLY IF YOU FEEL THE NEED)

SOCIAL MEDIA

Having spent so long talking about online dating websites, apps, the dos and don'ts, the pros and many, *many* cons, there's a part of me that wants to rip those pages out, and consign them to electronic oblivion. Not because I didn't enjoy writing them, and certainly not because I don't believe the advice is sound – this is how the world works (at least right now, March 2018) – but times, they are a changing.

Here's a prediction for you. Five years from now, dating *websites* as they exist today – dedicated portals for 'singles' to create profiles, browse profiles, and send messages into the void, all in the hopes of finding romance – will be gone. And good riddance too, because what will replace them has the potential to change dating forever.

Even in the few years this book has been available I've noticed more and more of the traditional dating sites lifting concepts such as 'friends', and 'likes', and 'comments', and 'shares', from mainstream social media platforms and incorporating them into their own sites. Why? Because when it comes to encouraging people to interact with others in a virtual environment – the very thing that dating sites are *supposed* to do well – social media does it a whole load better.

In fact when you think about it, social media has a lot going for it as an online dating medium: It's usually free, easy to use, there are LOADS of people on it, and most of them are actually real. More than that, *unlike* the dating sites, it's far easier to strike up a conversation with someone on *Facebook* and *Twitter*. Being involved in a discussion you find mutually interesting is *how* you meet people in the first place – the ice is already broken.

Now, it has to be said, I use social media primarily to reach new readers; promoting myself as an author and therefore my books. Its secondary purpose, so I tell everyone, is to allow me to interact with my *existing* readers without whom I wouldn't have a job. What I actually mean by that is that I'm basically just messing about whilst I avoid doing the work that an author should be doing. But, strange though it may seem, were I going to use social media to meet new people with the hopes of snaring a date I wouldn't really do anything different. My underlying strategy would be *exactly* the same; be interesting, entertaining, chatty, positive, open, and prepared to talk to anyone, everyone, and (occasionally) no one, about anything and everything.

What follows then are a few pointers on how to go about doing exactly that.

I'm primarily going to talk about *Facebook* because:

- It's the biggest social media site there is
- The vast majority of users are adults (rather than teenagers)
- It's one I consider myself something of an expert on.

That said, any of the principals here should translate to most other social media networks, such as *Twitter* or *Google+* if they're your bag. If you find the advice on the following pages *doesn't* apply to your social media site of choice it might be time to give in to the dark side and join us on *Facebook*.

I'm also going to assume a basic knowledge of social media (and *Facebook*, in particular). If you're completely new to these platforms… ask a friend, a work colleague, or a teenager, or indeed anybody, to show you around!

The Basics

Just like regular dating websites, your primary objective is to interact with as many (new) people as possible, and to get to a point where you're exchanging private messages, before you eventually propose 'coffee'.

If you're already an avid user of social media this might be a slight shift in mindset. Social media is extremely good at mimicking real life and allowing communities to develop, and most social media users will stay within these communities, conversing only with their friends – be they real friends or *Facebook* 'friends'. That's not going to work for us. From hereon we're going to be interacting with total strangers and doing anything we can to reach as many 'friends of friends' as possible.

This being the case a detailed review of your profile would be extremely prudent.

Let's start by keeping you safe: Be careful about revealing your actual date of birth (at the very least ditch the year you were born), and the exact location of where you live. Remove or hide your email address, and telephone number. If your phone / tablet knows exactly where you are and is in the habit of automatically feeding this information to the web, switch it off! This includes your phone's camera. You basically want to remove any information that might be useful to a hacker, spammer, scammer, or fraudster. Don't be seduced by that 'friends only' option that allows you to hide personal information from everyone but your nearest and dearest. It takes just one click to make someone a 'friend', but it could take several days to discover someone isn't quite as friendly as you initially thought. If you're not comfortable with the *whole world* knowing something, it *shouldn't* be on your profile.

Now let's get more positive. Take a look at what you have in the 'about you' / 'bio' text. If it's blank (as is so often the case with people on *Facebook*) this is a missed opportunity. Pen a quick paragraph summing up who you are and what you're about. Here's a good one I found on *Twitter*.

> Foodie chick. Flavour lover. Traveller, Gym Bunny. Avid Telly watcher. Reader of inspirational book stuff

And another:

> I'm 95 years young. I don't repeat myself. My dog Sebastian gets me, my children aren't even on Twitter! I'm 95 years young. I'm a champion quilter & baker. I'm 95.

Notice how our social media bio is all me me me me me. And that's just fine. Preferable, in fact. Telling the world that we're looking for Prince Charming is expected on *TiredOfKissingFrogs.com*, here on *Facebook/Twitter* it'll come across as slightly desperate – it might also attract people we'd rather keep at arm's length.

Which brings me rather nicely on to the thorny issue of your 'relationship' status: Leave it blank. Or set it to 'only me' (so that it's effectively invisible to anyone but you). You might think broadcasting your single status to the world would be a good thing – the virtual equivalent of putting up a 'for sale' sign – it's not.

According to Doctor Robert Cialdini[31] we're naturally attracted to things *other* people want (the principal of 'social proof'; if other people think this thing is good, then it must be good), as well as those things we can't have (the principal of scarcity; "for a limited time only" or "sold out"). I'd like to propose that the inverse of these principals might also be true, in that being perceived as both 'available' and 'no one else wants you' are *unattractive* qualities. And I would know.

When I met my wife she was extremely suspicious of my 'single' status. She was convinced that I was either married, still in love with an ex-girlfriend, seeing someone secretly, or an axe murderer. It

---

[31] Entertaining public speaker and author of *'Influence – Science and Practice'*.

didn't make any sense to her that I was thirty-something, without having gone through a messy divorce at least once, and without having spawned any children. The only possible explanation was there was something about me that other women found off-putting – something that she hadn't figured out yet. It simply didn't occur to her that I was just completely rubbish at meeting women.

Now, I wouldn't go as far to suggest you change your *Facebook* status to say you're 'married' when you're not, but a degree of ambiguity might not necessarily be a bad thing.

Photos

Many social media sites allow you to keep virtual photo albums. It's not unusual for someone to have several hundred pictures of themselves for all the world to see. On some social media platforms (*Instagram, Pinterest, Tumblr...*) it's all about the pictures, and how you see the world.

Potentially, this is a very good thing. The more pictures there are of you going about your fantastic life, having a good time, and generally looking like the sort of person someone would want to spend time with, the better – but be careful. Take a virtual step backwards and browse through those pictures. Taken as a whole what do they say about you? Does it look like you spend most of your day taking 'selfies' in the bathroom mirror? Or every evening at a bar somewhere? Or lying facedown on the pavement outside a bar somewhere? Are you usually pictured draped round someone of the opposite sex? Do you instinctively pull a face when someone points a camera at you? If so, it might be time to delete a few photos, or better still add some others to create a little balance.

Remember, also, that on *Facebook* people have the ability to 'tag' you in their own photos, effectively adding a picture of you which you might not want public.

Finally, think carefully about the picture you choose as your profile picture (the thumbnail that will appear next to every comment you make). It's the first picture that people will see – make sure it's a good one.

For more on what to put / not to put on your profile in the way of text or photographs, re-read the previous chapters and sections on choosing your photos and writing a self summary. Whilst these chapters were specifically written with dating sites in mind, many of the principals discussed are just as valid here. In the meantime, however, let's sum up what we've learnt so far.

STOP! ACTION POINT!

Social Media – the basics

Review your profile. Consider the following:

- Remove anything that could be used by a scammer, spammer, hacker or fraudster.
- Write a short, witty, friendly 'about me' bio.
- Hide your relationship status.
- Review your photos.

Working 'Social Media'

So, having cleaned up our profile, we're ready to start strutting our stuff, and doing all that we can to 'meet' new people.

Here are some do's and don'ts.

The Do's...

Do post everything (pictures, comments, status updates, links) as 'public'. You want *everyone* to be able to see anything you write. But think carefully before you hit enter. This is PUBLIC. Really public. Much more public even than standing in the middle of the high street with a megaphone held to your mouth. Every saucy comment, every flirt, every smiley face, every 'like', every bad word, every drunken picture of you, can – and possibly will – be seen by everyone. Including your mum. And Father Patrick. And the police. And the daily newspapers. More than that, depending on the way your friends and followers have their *Facebook* settings set, anything you type, 'share' or 'like' might instantly be sent, *via email*, to any number of people. Sure, *Facebook* gives you the ability to 'unlike' something, delete or edit a comment – but that's pretty much cosmetic. *Facebook* is sending a million[32] emails out every minute of the day – that's a lot of horses that have already bolted. You know that dream you sometimes have about being naked in the office? *Facebook* is like that. Worse actually, because *Facebook* does a very good job of convincing you that you're *not* actually naked, whilst everyone looks on and wonders why you got that embarrassing tattoo.

Do be friendly.

Do be active. Like stuff. Comment. But...

Do be discerning. Don't be that person who likes and comments on *everything* before anyone else.

---

[32] Probably.

Most important of all – do be social. Rather than limiting yourself to your 'friends' and their 'friends', seek out *Facebook* groups and pages as a way to 'meet' new people. There's a group or page for pretty much anything you can think of (people, places, books... everything!) – all full of people chatting about the thing they have in common.

And finally, do enjoy yourself. If you're not having fun, you're not doing it right.

The Don'ts...

Don't send random 'friend' requests to everyone you like the look of. It looks weird. It *is* weird. You need to get to a point where you're exchanging *comments*. More on this in a moment.

Don't be negative. No moaning. No whingeing. No ranting. No slagging off the opposite sex. You've had a bad day? Keep it to yourself. You want some sympathy? Call your mum, or your best pal – *Facebook* isn't the place for that.

Don't be a sleazeball. Your friends *might* find your saucy sense of humour hilarious, total strangers probably won't. There's a huge difference between being friendly, flirty, and a letch.

Above all: Don't trust the privacy settings.

How Facebook works

Ironically, having warned you about how utterly public *Facebook* is, one of the biggest misconceptions people have is that whilst pretty much anyone *can* see anything you've ever put on *Facebook*, some assume that their 'friends' will *always* see *everything* they post. So, whilst you could write "having a party tonight at my place – eight till late – everyone invited" there's every chance that come ten p.m. you'll be on your tod, with nothing but a pile of vol au vents to keep you company – which would be a shame as I'm particularly fond of vol au vents.

Your lack of guests probably has nothing to do with you or your vol au vents, and everything to do with the fact that nobody ever saw your *Facebook* post. And why would this be?

What few people realise is that the items that make up your *Facebook* news feed (the list of 'posts' you're presented with when you log in) are broadly speaking determined by four things:

- Who you're friends with, who you're 'following', and what you've liked.
- The *individual* settings for each of your friends, people you follow, or pages you've liked (for instance, you can exclude updates from certain friends or pages or groups in your news feed).
- How *popular Facebook* deems that post. A post's popularity is determined by the number of comments, shares and likes it receives.
- What the post actually is. Broadly speaking *Facebook loves* pictures, *hates* links[33], and is generally neutral about text-only updates.

So whether I see your party invite depends on whether I'm your friend or following you, whether I've chosen to see your updates in my news feed, how popular that post is compared to others *Facebook* is putting in front of me, and whether your invite was a caption on a picture, a link that would take me away from *Facebook*, or plain text.

And here's the kicker – you have very little control over any of that.

Or do you?

Were I attempting to promote a party on *Facebook* I'd start by finding an amusing photo (that people might share), and post it (publicly) with a caption that encourages a response, such as "party at my place? Eight till late? Who's coming?" The subsequent shares, likes and comments *should* increase the popularity of the post meaning that more and more people will actually see it.

By way of example here's a post that I put on *Facebook* and *Twitter* yesterday which was unusually successful. It was text only and read...

---

[33] It's worth noting that a link to YouTube doesn't necessarily take someone away from *Facebook*, so this might be an exception to this rule.

> A friend suggested I try meditating and ask my higher self what I
> should focus on. My higher self said "cake". Wise words indeed.

It was an off-the-cuff remark but it generated numerous comments,
likes, and re-tweets. This one post led to several new people
following me on both platforms.

The day before this was my *Facebook* status update:

> Damn mosquito bites! Anybody know how to stop 'em itching?

Within 24 hours I had 22 comments, three of which are from
'friends of friends' – people I don't actually know. That's three
people I should seriously consider 'friending'.

Making 'friends'

Virtually all social media sites work by creating a network of people
who are linked to each other. On *Twitter* and *Instagram* we 'follow'
each other. On *Facebook* we 'friend' people – but we can also
'follow'. On *LinkedIn* we add 'connections' – which is ironic as
there's nothing about *LinkedIn* that doesn't make me want to get as
far away from it as possible.

Some of these platforms (such as a *Facebook* 'friend request')
require both parties to agree to the connection. Others (such as the
Twitter 'follow') do not. Either way, the more 'friends' and 'followers'
you have, the further your 'reach' becomes. Somewhere out there,
amongst your 'friends of friends', the 'followers' of your 'followers',
might be a potential date. The bigger your network, the more likely
that scenario becomes.

With this in mind, making 'friends' and encouraging 'followers' is
crucial to your success.

One of the good things about *Twitter*, *Instagram* and sites where
people 'follow' you, is that the only way to get 'followers' is to
become someone that people *want* to follow – by being friendly,
funny, entertaining and/or informative. On *Facebook*, *LinkedIn* and
other sites where you request 'friendship' it's all too easy to send that
request before you've done the groundwork. And really, you need to

get to a point where a friend request isn't going to appear weird. How do you know where that point is?

Personally, if I'm exchanging *comments* with someone on a regular basis *then* I'd feel comfortable sending a friend request.

It's worth pointing out (again) that 'friends' and 'followers' are a good thing. They extend your reach. Don't fall into the trap of *only* 'friending' people you might be prepared to date. We're not at that stage yet. Even if you wouldn't 'friend' this person in real life, it may still be worth sending a request.

A quick word on incoming 'friend' requests. If you're playing the social media game effectively, eventually people are going to want to 'friend' you. Again, this is mostly a good thing BUT let's be smart about this. Be extremely suspicious of requests from people you don't recognise. Before you click 'accept' have a quick look at the friends you have in common to see if you can figure out how they found you. Social media feels a lot safer than some of the dating sites, but be warned, it still has more than its fair share of weirdoes, trolls and other internet hoodlums.

Finding a potential and sending that first message

Eventually, after all the sharing and liking and commenting and tweeting and retweeting… you're going to stumble across someone who you'd rather interact with in a way that doesn't require technical wizardry.

However, whilst everyone who's ever used a *dating* site expects to get out-of-the-blue messages from strangers – and then doesn't! – no one *ever* expects to get out-of-the-blue messages on a site that's been labelled 'social media'. That's irony for you.

In fact *Facebook* does a rather good job of filtering messages from 'strangers' and hiding them away so that you'll never ever see them. *Twitter* actively encourages its users to flag spammers. Other social media platforms do similar things. And quite right too. All of which means you have to adopt a slightly different approach before sending that first message.

For starters (assuming we're still talking about *Facebook*) you should aim to be 'friends' *before* you send your message[34] (see above). Once you're 'friends' you might suddenly have access to a whole load of information that you previously couldn't see (such as their 'about' page, photos, etc). Do a background check (just as you would on a regular dating site – see previous chapters), before sending a short, chummy, opening message (again, just as you would on a regular dating site).

Once you've sent your message you might want to adopt the same 'send and forget' ethos as discussed earlier in the book. Send. And forget. Don't go sending chaser messages, just wait.

To save yourself future heartache, just as we removed profiles from our list of favourites on dating sites, so it might be a good idea to hide someone on *Facebook* after we've sent that initial message. To do this, put your mouse pointer over their name *without* clicking. A pop up box should appear. Navigate carefully through the options such that you no longer see their updates in your timeline[35]. Do this properly, and you'll still be 'friends', you'll still see a reply should you get one, but in the meantime you won't be driven crazy seeing all their *Facebook* activity whilst they seemingly ignore you.

On the flip side you might get an answer to your message immediately, perhaps even whilst you're online. One of the oddities of *Facebook* messaging is that it tends to straddle the boundaries between 'emailing' and 'instant messaging', and what started as a well thought out message can suddenly become an on-screen 'chat'.

Let's take some action!

---

[34] In Twitter terms you need to be following each other before you can exchange direct messages.

[35] I'm being intentionally vague here because *Facebook* has a habit of regularly changing the way it works.

STOP! ACTION POINT!

Working Social Media

- Be friendly.
- Be active (like, comment, share).
- Be social. (Join pages. Join groups. Join in).
- Post everything as public.
- Remember that it's PUBLIC.
- Don't trust the privacy settings.
- Don't send random 'friend' requests.
- Don't be negative or sleazy.
- Make friends with anyone you've exchanged comments with (not just with those you fancy).

Remember:

- Facebook likes pictures.
- is neutral about text.
- hates links.

Only private message those people you're actually friends with!

- Keep it short, light, and friendly.
- Send and forget.

If you're not having fun, you're not doing it right.

SPEED DATING

Many many months ago, I strode into the offices of a rather large publisher to chat about this book, and the sample chapters I'd sent them.

They were, I think it's fair to say, delighted. Although they weren't that keen on the title.

Originally this book was going to be called *'How To Survive Online Dating'*. I thought it was apt. You know those war movies where the hero spends most of his time crawling around in mud, trying to stay out of sight, dodging barbed wire, whilst being rained on with bits of exploding tanks and burnt flesh? Sometimes online dating can feel a bit like that. Sometimes. Or, to put it another way, when one morning you finally wake up next to someone warm and beautiful you can't help but feel like you've *'survived'*.

My publisher however thought the word 'Survival' was a little negative. More than that, they'd done some research and it turns out the 'online dating' book market is a little too niche, and not as big as the *'general* dating' book market. Could I perhaps come up with a different title? A title with the same rhythm as my other two books? Oh, and could I drop the word 'online', and make it a little more *general?*

Well – I was flummoxed. Changing the title was one thing, but almost every romance I've embarked upon in the last few years has been as a direct result of punching some words into a computer and posting them on the world wide web. Those that weren't, come under the general heading of 'happy accident' (a chapter we'll come to in a few pages time).

Truth is, despite appearances, I'm not the most social of animals. I don't like clubs or crowded bars. I pretty much hate parties of all descriptions. And as such I've never been very good at any form of dating that involves walking up to complete strangers.

I've considered it. Of course I have. I've actually read a number of 'pick-up guides'[36]. Most of them have been surprisingly instructive – especially on *actual* dates – but not one has ever persuaded me that I could have improved my odds of romance by leaving the safety of my desk, and venturing into 'the field'.

That's not to say that there isn't a half-way house. An off-line dating experience that's a little more structured than simply throwing yourself to the wolves. If you've had enough of my obsession with websites, photos, self-summaries, and what to say in your 'opening message', then pick out a pair of funky jeans, that shirt everyone says you look good in, put on your broadest smile and prepare for one of the most hectic, but none-the-less fun evenings, you're ever likely to have.

Speed dating might be just what you're looking for.

---

[36] Books aimed at fellas wanting to learn how to 'pick-up' a date in a bar, nightclub, or public situation.

What Is Speed Dating?

Allegedly dreamt up by a Rabbi in Los Angeles as a way for Jewish singles to meet each other, a 'Speed Dating' event aims to set you up with perhaps a dozen really quick dates during the course of one evening, and afterwards lets you know whether any of the dates you took a fancy to share that attraction.

Your standard event starts with participants being coupled at random and sat at a table for two. A bell rings to signify that you have just three minutes[37] to chat and generally make a good impression. When it rings again, one person remains seated (in a heterosexual event this is usually the woman) whilst the other party moves to the next table. The process repeats until everyone has met their potential dates.

During the course of the evening you're expected to jot down on a score card which of your dates you'd like to see again, and which you'll be hiding from should you spot them in the local supermarket. The organisers collect the score cards and notify you (usually the next day) of your 'matches' (those people you fancied, who also took a shine to you), along with their contact details.

What happens then is left to you.

---

[37] Some events allow longer. Nine minutes is the longest I've ever heard of.

What *Actually* Happens

I've been to four speed dating events. Three as a participant, and one as a 'friend'[38].

The first event was something of a damp squib (though at the time I thought it was going quite well). Aside from the usual nerves I was pretty sure I knew what to expect. I stood at the bar with the other guys, trying not to look too hard at the large group of ladies huddled in the corner, many of whom were glancing in our direction and already seemed to be somewhat disappointed. I noticed there were more women than men, and later realised that was because at least a third of them were 'friends' who wouldn't be taking part in the actually dating process.

Amongst my 'competitors' (because let's face it, that's what they were) were two men who'd been to similar events before. One man had broken up with his girlfriend of six months only the week before. He'd met her at a previous speed dating event, and was here to find her replacement. The other, an incredibly tall and quiet man, reluctantly admitted that he attended speed dating events "quite often". In fact I later discovered he was well known to the organisers. He was their regular. Just before we took our places I sneaked a look at his score card and noticed that he'd already said yes to everyone.

I learnt three important things that evening.

Firstly, three minutes isn't long at all. It's barely enough time to get seated, introduce yourself, comment on how mad the evening is and then get bogged down in each others work lives.

That's the second thing.

If you let a conversation take its natural course, within thirty seconds you're asking each other what you do for a living and this

---

[38] It's quite common for people to take a friend. Usually they hang around at the bar.

isn't necessarily a good thing. Not when that thing is the stunningly dull world of *credit card banking*.

And my third epiphany of the evening?

Three minutes is enough. It's ample time to work out if you fancy someone, discover whether there might be a spark of attraction between you... and then snuff it out with two and a half minutes of boring work-talk.

Despite this, I remained positive.

I figured that there were very few ladies in the room I wouldn't consider seeing again, at least for another date. Somewhere a little less rushed, where I'd have ample opportunity to reveal just how interesting I could be. With this in mind, I indicated on my score card that I'd be prepared to meet seven out of the ten women from the evening.

The following day I received an email from the organiser. I had zero matches.

I was crushed.

How could that be?

But once I'd drowned my sorrows for an evening I came to the conclusion that it *wasn't me.* Or at least, it wasn't *entirely* me. Speed dating was a game. And games can be mastered.

Less than a month later I was back for a second attempt. This time, I knew what to expect. I'd researched possible questions on the internet. I'd spent the day practicing on my female colleagues. And I'd figured out how I was going to answer the 'work' question. I was ready.

I also persuaded a female friend to come with me which at the time seemed like a great idea (in that I was less nervous) but in retrospect may have been a bit foolish (in that I reduced my potential matches from ten to nine). It did mean, however, that I didn't have to talk to the incredibly tall quiet man. Yes. He was back. Last time hadn't worked out so well for him either.

I fared considerably better. By the end of the night I'd selected half a dozen potential matches of which two selected me back.

That should have been the end of my speed dating days. But this is real life. Nothing is that simple, and neither match ever made it to that 'second' date.

The first confessed over the phone that she'd been so drunk she'd completely forgotten to score anyone. At the end of her evening, in a moment of inebriated panic, she just ticked all the boxes on her card and as a consequence I was one of several similar conversations she'd had that day. I suggested that maybe we could go for a second date anyway but she wasn't keen. Thinking about it now, I wonder just how true any of her story actually was.

As for the other match, well it was me who was less than enthusiastic. Of the six ladies I'd chosen, this one was most definitely bottom of my list. Had I not met the other five ladies – four of whom had chosen to put an X next to my name, and the other of which had rejected me due to an alcohol induced technicality – I'd probably have been happily dialling her number and inviting her out, but here I was, her phone number in my hand, and all I could think of was how I was getting the bottom of the barrel. To my shame I never followed it up.

I felt both better and worse when neither did she.

You'd think that these two incidents might be enough to put me off speed dating but no, a couple of months later I was back. Third time's a charm, so they say.

Once again I took a female friend, and once again the tall, quiet man skulked in the corner and ticked all the boxes before we'd even begun. But this time round, my entire attitude had changed.

This time rather than treat each 'date' like some sort of vetting process – a three minute audition to see whether we'd like to progress to another meet-up – I decided that I was only going to select those ladies that I *really* liked. Ladies that I could see myself having some sort of relationship with. Yes, there might have to be a second 'date', but that wasn't my intention. My intention was to *select a girlfriend*.

In addition to this, I also adopted a far more relaxed, almost cynical approach. The first two events hadn't been particularly successful, I had no reason to suspect that this would either. But now I knew exactly what to expect. I could just keep coming back as many times as I liked. Odds were I'd only get better, surely? Only the presence of the incredibly tall, quiet man, made me unsure that this was actually the case.

At the end of the evening I'd selected just three ladies out of the nine. The following day I discovered they'd all matched.

Speed Dating Tips & Tricks

So then, if none of that has put you off the idea, here's how to get the best out of speed dating.

Finding your event

Finding a proper speed dating event can be a challenge. A quick *Google* search will present many *many* results, but annoyingly, most of these may turn out to be general singles nights, events listing sites, or online dating companies. You may have to ask around, or extend your search to include your nearest city.

Some speed dating events are run by the large online dating companies – and some of those are the *same* companies who the BBC accused of routinely creating hoax profiles. Now, clearly I'm not suggesting that they hire actors or actresses for their speed dating events, but given the choice between one of their events and another run by an independent company, I know which I would choose.

There is nearly always a fee. And it isn't always cheap.

Remember that the organisers need your contact details to send you your matches the following day, but keep in mind that these might be added to a mailing list. It might be worth creating a unique email address which you can later ditch when the spam starts arriving.

Events can often be 'themed' – in the sense that you have events for people in their twenties, their thirties, their forties, or for people with a shared interest in a topic.

One of the most crazy speed dating variations I've come across was a company that introduced a third 'friends only' column to the score card. Now, theoretically, this is a nice idea; you meet someone you kind of click with, but you're not sure there's any chemistry, so you tick the 'friends' box instead of the 'never darken my door again' box.

Mathematically, however, this additional option significantly *decreases* your chances of getting any matches whatsoever. My advice would be, a) steer clear of events organised this way or, b) mark anyone you like the look of as both a possible relationship AND a friend.

During the event

Most events are fairly casual, so unless stated otherwise, dress as if you were meeting someone for coffee (more on this in a few chapters time).

Personally, I find the waiting around at the start excruciating. If I were any good at walking up to complete strangers and engaging them in conversation then this entire book would have probably concentrated on the art of meeting people in public places. Instead, I recommend taking a friend so you don't have to pretend to play with your phone or admire the paintings on the wall for long periods of time.

Throughout the evening stay focused. Despite appearances, this isn't a social event – this is 'work'. You're here to find a date. All the time and effort that you might have spent on internet dating has been distilled into one intense evening. So, either buy one drink at the start and make it last all night, or stick to the soft drinks.

Your 'dates' will go far better if *you* lead the conversation. You'll come across as confident and interesting, and yet all it actually requires is a little mental preparation beforehand.

For instance, unless you have a particularly fascinating job, avoid talking about work – talk about your interests instead. Even if you *do* have a particularly interesting job (maybe you're a pilot, a trapeze artist, or an author – something exciting like that), move on to something else as quickly as possible. 'Work' is a boring rut that's too easy to get stuck in, and quite frankly you don't have the time.

Here are a few ways to sidestep the work question, or make it more interesting;

"I'm a {civil engineer} during the day, but by night I'm a {dance instructor}".

"Tell you what, why don't you try and guess what I do for a living – I'll give you three guesses and then I'll tell you which one was the closest" – follow this up with – "Okay, my turn..."

"Let's not talk about work, tell me what you like to do for fun..."

Another example of leading the conversation is to have a few fun questions squirreled away at the back of your mind. Here are few of my favourites;

"Baths or showers?"
"Cats or dogs?"
"Favourite food?"
"If you could travel anywhere in the world where would it be?"
"If you were a pizza, what sort of topping would you have and why?" (Be prepared to jump in with your own answer to this one – most people draw a blank the moment they're asked this).

Remember to score people as you go. Generally, the most polite way to do this is as you (or your date) are moving between tables. Remember to be discerning (choose people you'd happily embark on a relationship with), but not 'ridiculously picky'. Set yourself a rule that you *will* select at least one person. Try and be objective. If height is a show stopper for you, well, so be it. But what hand they write with might be a step too far. As is their choice of shoes.

Whilst we're on the subject, make your *own* choices. Generally, at these dos there's a break at half time, and what I've noticed is that the women retreat to the toilets to compare notes. *This is bad news for everyone concerned.*

At my second speed dating event I'd been doing rather well with a short blonde. She'd been all giggles and smiles, playing with her hair as we spoke. I could have talked to her all night long. But at half time, whilst us fellas stood at the bar feeling quietly confident, my blonde was squeezed into toilet facilities that could barely cope with half a dozen people, let alone my eight other dates and their non-dating friends. According to *my* friend, as Blondie voiced her mutual admiration for me one of her so-called girly chums responded with "what, the writer bloke? Oo no!" – and the tick next to my name was quickly changed to a cross.

There are two morals to this tale. Firstly, unless your friends have specific reasons for not liking someone you were getting along just fine with, take their thoughts and feelings with a generous handful of salt. Remember, they're there to find a date too – *you're actually in competition*! Secondly, women hunt in packs. Not a single woman at that event or the others I attended came alone. Therefore it's not necessarily that easy to figure out who came with who. Regardless of who you ultimately put a tick next to on your score card it's important to win over *everyone*.

After the event

Remember it's not the quantity of matches that are important – it's the quality. You only need *one* good match.

Take a quick look at the first half of the title of this book – *don't wait for them to make contact!* Pick up the phone or send an email as soon as you can. Jump forward to the chapter entitled 'Phase Four' in the second half of this book.

STOP! ACTION POINT!

Speed Dating Events

Finding your event

- Pick your event of choice with care.
- Travel to your nearest city if you need to.
- Beware events that have a 'friends' option on their score cards.

Before the event:

- Have an answer ready for the 'work' question.
- Prepare some good questions in your head.

During:

- Stay focused: one alcoholic drink only.
- Lead the conversation.
- Get off the topic of work or avoid it completely.
- Select only people you really like.

Women have a tendency to hunt in packs. So,

- Men: it's important to win over everyone.
- Women: consider being a lone wolf.

After:

- Don't wait. Make contact.

ACCIDENTAL DATING

So, how's it all going? Please tell me that you have at least got yourself an online dating profile, that you're sending messages, that you're flirting on *Facebook*, or that you're booked into a speed dating event? Need I remind you that reading this book – I mean *just* reading, without following through on any of the Action Points – won't actually achieve anything? Of course I don't. You know that. You're a smart cookie. You probably have every intention of taking some of the advice in these here pages just as soon as, well, just as soon as you've got tomorrow out the way. Because who knows, tomorrow might be *the day*! The day when Mr or Ms Lovely Person sits themselves next to you, on the bus, or the train, at the morning marketing meeting, or in that poetry seminar you almost didn't bother going to. They glance in your direction, you catch their eye, and the rest of your life – the happy ever after you've been waiting for – just *unfolds*.

Now there's a part of me, a big part of me, that wants to shake you by the shoulders and tell you to get over it! Life just doesn't work that way! But remember Jon and Gina from chapter one? That's *exactly* how life worked out for them. And whilst they're the exception rather than the norm, nobody wants to be the norm. We'd all rather be the exception.

Originally, this was going to be a tough love chapter, an entire section dedicated to telling you how I don't believe it's possible to engineer accidental relationships. They are, by their very nature, *accidents* – chance encounters, that lead to something more. But what I actually believe is that every single conundrum on the planet has a solution, and whilst 'chance encounters' still rely on chance, you can significantly increase your odds of having one.

Do you remember how I met Kate (I talked about it back in the opening chapter)? It wasn't just about signing up for a flirting course and sitting myself next to the prettiest girl in the room: prior to that, you'll remember, I also underwent something of a self imposed image makeover.

Now, I'm not about to start handing out fashion advice or makeup tips. That's not my bag. There also isn't enough room in this book. What definitely *is* my bag, however, is a slew of ideas based on my own experience and/or scientific research, on how you can influence and improve how people perceive you. Think of it as a step-by-step personal re-branding exercise, wrapped up in its own mini-book, that can not only improve your overall dating success rate, but can yield impressive results on their own; seemingly increasing those chance encounters, and turning you into a 'accidental relationship' waiting to happen.

If you've been following my advice, but you're yet to successfully get beyond a first date, or if you've enjoyed what you've read so far but you'd prefer to try something a little less gung-ho, then I encourage you to take a look at the short companion guide to this book: *'How To Be Even More Attractive[39]*. It's available in paperback, as an e-book, and comes free with the audio version of this book.

Visit HowToBeEvenMoreAttractive.com for more details.

In the meantime, let's talk 'dates'.

---

[39] Originally published as *'From Invisible To Irresistible'*

Part 2

"You and me, Babe –
how about it?"

DATES

Well, hello there. Fancy meeting you here. What's a lovely reader, such as yourself, doing in this part of the book? Could it be that you were steadily working your way through Part 1, when – *bam!* – one of your potentials suddenly agreed to meet you for coffee? Would that be about right?

Or have you actually been sitting there in that armchair, chuckling away, ignoring the Action Points, whilst working your way through a packet of biscuits? Hmmmm?

Either way, the next few chapters deal with the thorny issue of *dating* – by which I mean *real* dates, in the real world. It's time to turn that computer off and don your best frock. Maybe.

If Part One of this book was all about *finding* potentials, Part Two – this part – is about finding out whether a potential who's shown some degree of promise could be something more. It's about taking things one step further, then another step, and then another step, until – if you're of a mind – you can quit dating altogether!

I've broken these steps into seven phases which should take you from *coffee* to *date number three* – after that you're on your own! I say 'should' because in my experience it's a rare thing to get from phase one to phase seven without a hitch, and without having to start again. But that's the nature of the game, and if you think of it *as a game*, you'll enjoy it more and be a lot more successful.

Let's recap on where you are right now.

Phase One: Initial Messages

We covered messages back in Part One. Jump back for more detail on what to say, what not to say, message length, and so on and so forth. The important thing to keep in mind is that you're trying to achieve two things with your messages:

- Develop a little rapport.
- Arrange a coffee date by the third or fourth message.

Remember. Keep all your messages 'inside' the dating site or social media medium of your choosing. Don't go handing over your email address, mobile phone number, or other personal information. Aside from the fact you don't know this person well enough you want to avoid making your message exchange too convenient. Bat one too many flirty messages back and forth and you run the risk of creating the 'pleasant message exchange'– seductive though that may be, they rarely end in relationships.

If the other person tells you that they can't access the dating site from work – or some other reason why email or text messaging would be far more convenient – use that as leverage to bring the next stage forwards; what's a more effective form of communication than real words, in the real world, perhaps over a lovely warm beverage? How about we meet for coffee? Tomorrow lunchtime? Or after work?

Phase One (b): The Phone Call

Sometimes, either you, or your potential date, need more than messages to feel comfortable enough to commit to coffee. Sometimes it requires a phone call.

Now this runs slightly counter to the 'don't hand over any personal information before you meet rule', because unless you can find a public callbox, one of you is going to have to trust the other person with a telephone number.

Personally, I like to be the one doing the calling because I'm a control freak, and I don't want to have to wait in all night for a phone call that might never come. But whether you're making or receiving the call, make sure you're using a number you have some control over, should – heaven forbid – your potential turn out to have 'stalker qualities'. Personally, I use my home landline. It discourages text messages (for the reasons we discussed earlier), and it doesn't accept inbound calls from withheld numbers. I wouldn't go this far myself, but perhaps a pay-as-you-go sim card, that can be dumped if needs be, isn't such a bad idea.

So what should you talk about? Anything. Everything. I like to keep it light, and breezy. A verbal continuation of your online messages. If you're stuck, ask how their day's been so far – if they've had a good one ask a few questions. If they haven't, change the subject quickly and talk about yours. At this stage, what you talk about is far less important than the fact you're talking. Verbal communication takes things to a whole new level. You can tell a lot from the way a person talks, or rather your subconscious can. Within moments, you'll have a pretty good idea as to whether there's any chemistry between you and whether, or not, you should proceed to the next phase – which is, just so we're absolutely clear on this point, *coffee*.

Unless you're both really enjoying yourself try not to talk for too long. If needs be, go ring the doorbell and bring the conversation to a close, or have somewhere you need to be. Better to leave them wanting more, but before you do, if the conversation's going well, you want to be arranging coffee.

Notice again, that we're *not* handing out our email address, or mobile number. Seductive though that may be, it's a slippery slope. If 'coffee' goes well, *then* you can email, text, message and phone each other to your heart's delight. But not before.

If your phone chat *isn't* going that well, well then, it's time to adopt the doorbell trick again, and bring the conversation to a swift close with a polite 'thanks for calling,' or 'thanks for the chat'. Don't make promises, or excuses – just be polite, put a smile in your voice, and end the conversation. Then chalk it up to experience and move on. Most of all though, *do not* arrange to meet in the hopes that they'll seem more interesting in person. They won't. Trust your instincts. They're nearly always right.

STOP! ACTION POINT!

The Phone Call.

- If you need a phone conversation to achieve the level of comfort necessary to arrange a meet-up, remember the following:

- Use a number you have some level of control over.

- Keep the conversation light and breezy.

- If things are going well, arrange coffee (see Phase Two)!

- If things aren't going well, bring conversation to a swift, polite close.

Phase Two: Arrange Coffee

Let's assume that you're still on the phone, and you're definitely hitting it off. Or that you've reached message three or four and things are going great.

Time to arrange 'coffee'.

Why coffee?

What do you mean *"why coffee?"* Where were you when we discussed this earlier?

'Coffee' is the smart dater's alternative to a first date!

Nobody likes first dates. There's far too much pressure and expectation riding on them – all bundled together into a stressful, potentially expensive night out, preceded by an afternoon of worrying about it. The only useful elements of a first date are:

- You finally get to see what your potential *really* looks like.

- You get to hear their voice.

- You discover whether or not there's any chemistry between you, and…

- You build more rapport.

..and all of that can be achieved in thirty minutes, over coffee. What's more, because 'coffee' is significantly less stressful neither one of you is likely to cock anything up!

Trust me, meeting for 'coffee' was one of the best tips I was ever given and I'm returning the favour by giving it to you.

Of course, you and I are in the minority when it comes to this 'coffee' business. Most of the world seems to believe that when meeting someone for the first time, 'dinner', or 'drinks' is the way to go. It's not. That's a first date. Which we're going to avoid. But what do you do if, having suggested coffee, your potential counters with an invite to this great little restaurant or pub that they know? Tell them you think that's a great idea, and you should meet for coffee to discuss it!

Chances are, however, that the 'coffee' suggestion will be met with much enthusiasm. In all my years of dating, I can, in actual fact, only ever remember one lady who insisted that we met for dinner. The rest saw 'coffee' for what it was. A quick, convenient, fun way to meet, for the first time.

If possible, you want to dictate the venue. Few things are more frustrating than a 'where shall we meet' conversation, and frustrating conversations is definitely something to avoid in these crucial early stages. Whereas, if you have somewhere in mind you'll come across as cool and confident. It also gives you more control over what happens *after* coffee.

If your favourite venue isn't convenient however, don't panic. Simply establish a mutually convenient area that you can both get to (say, a tube station), then use *Google Maps* and 'streetview' to find the nearest coffee venue.

Good coffee venues

So what makes a good coffee venue?

Though it may sound obvious the best place for coffee is a proper coffee place such as Starbucks, or Café Nero, or a good quality independent. Though most of these places usually have big squashy sofas make sure your place has a selection of tables and chairs. Better to be sitting opposite each other, leaning forwards across a small round table – or side by side on the bar stools by the window – rather than miles apart and disappearing down the back of an arm chair. Also, those hard chairs get uncomfortable after a while, which believe it or not is a good thing. You *don't* want 'coffee' to last all afternoon. It's coffee. Thirty minutes to an hour. Max.

An alternative to a coffee shop might be a small café of some description, but avoid a restaurant – big or small. You don't want this to turn into lunch or dinner – at least not without *your* say so.

Most of all though, avoid meeting in a pub. Yes, these days, pubs do indeed serve coffee. They also serve alcohol. Don't get me wrong, I'm not against the drinking of hard liquor, I've had many a successful date which featured such an activity, but for your initial meet-up you need to be sober, and to have your wits about you. Do this right and I promise you it'll be the most successful non-first-date of your life.

There's a particular branch of Starbucks I used to frequent. It's in central London so it's dead easy to get to, and, more importantly, find. It's only a few minutes walk from the tube and the mainline station where I used to catch my train home. It has great views of the River Thames – which is both charming, and makes for good conversation. But more than that it's only a stone's throw from several nice restaurants, pubs and bars (more on *that* in a moment).

Safety First

Having worked hard to keep ourselves safe online, it goes without saying that you should continue to take precautions now that you're venturing into the real world. For instance, whether you choose to arrange coffee or something else, your first meeting (and possibly the second) should ALWAYS be in a public place. Let a close friend know where you're going and why. Ask them to check up on you later in the evening and/or the following morning. Never leave your drink unattended. Use your own transportation or public transport (rather than accepting a lift), and absolutely no walks via alleyways or deserted streets.

Everybody clear? Good. Let's do some work.

STOP! ACTION POINT!

Find a coffee location for those non-first-dates

Preferably it should be:

- Somewhere you know.
- Somewhere easy to get to.
- Somewhere easy to find.
- With tables and chairs.
- And nearby pubs, and restaurants (that you're also familiar with).

Stay safe:

- Tell a friend where you're going and why.
- Get them to check up on you.
- Don't leave drinks or food unattended.
- Use your own transportation.
- Avoid alleyways and deserted streets

Phase Three: Coffee!

My God – this is it! Proper dating! Hurrah for you! I can't tell you how pleased I am. But let's not get cocky. It's still very early days, and there's work to be done.

Let's check the basics.

Firstly, use whatever system you have to remind yourself of the date. You might think there's no earthly way you'll forget it, but put it in your diary anyway, or set a reminder on your phone to remind you on the morning, and possibly the day before. Do it for me.

Secondly, when you get that reminder, send a cheery message to your potential, along the lines of "see you later today – looking forward to it!" Clearly, we're hoping that they're as excited as you are – that there's no way they could possibly forget – but why take the chance?

What to wear

So that's the first and second potential disaster averted, now let's tackle your wardrobe.

It's only coffee, so there's no need to don your best frock or get the tux out, but at the same time you want to avoid looking like you got dressed in a strong wind with the lights off. You should definitely make a bit of an effort – but without *looking* like you've made an effort. What you're shooting for is the appearance of someone who is pleasantly turned out, but still capable of walking past a mirror without stopping to admire themselves or make adjustments.

Now I fully accept this might be tricky.

It took me many years, and professional assistance, to master my 'image'. Until that point I really had no idea what I was doing, and I'd spend an hour or so trying to assemble an outfit from a wardrobe of bits and pieces that I'd acquired since I was allowed to buy my own clothes. An outfit that might increase my chances of igniting a little passion. Passion that might result in considerably less clothing – of both parties, not necessarily tonight, but at some point in the future. It was the clothing equivalent of trying to build a particle accelerator from a box of old pinball machine parts when I had only the vaguest notion of what a particle accelerator should look like or how it works.

If any of this is striking a chord, try not to panic. Simply pick out something that's both comfortable and you think you look good in, and/or enlist the help of a trusted friend[40].

And if all this talk about outfits has got you nervous let's deal with those fears.

Nerves and anxiety

Nerves are natural. It's one of the reasons 'first dates' are such a minefield. But this isn't a 'first date', it's coffee.

If you find yourself feeling anxious, or imagining hideous outcomes, take a moment or two to grab back control of your thoughts. Have a quick look at your potential's photos (if convenient) and picture them in your coffee shop, sitting opposite, smiling and having a good time. Run through some likely conversations in your head, all the time imagining a positive outcome.

This is something you can do in the car, in bed, at work, whilst shaving, brushing your teeth, anywhere, in fact. And whilst it might feel a little self-indulgent and fanciful it's actually a technique that many a professional sports person uses. They picture the jump, the match, the race, and run through it in their head over and over again, each time imagining a successful outcome. Meanwhile, the subconscious, which is unable to tell the difference between a real event and an imagined one, effectively learns that this is how this particular activity is supposed to play out. When the real event

---

[40] You can find more tips on mastering your image in the companion guide to this book; '*How To Be Even More Attractive*'. Available from where ever you purchased this book.

happens, the subconscious recognises it, and begins to expect the outcome it has rehearsed many, many times before.

In addition to 'mental programming' exercises, the homeopathic remedy Gelsemium has been used by actors the world over to control stage fright, and Omega 3 Fish Oil capsules are proven to reduce stress.

Get there early

Leave plenty of time to get to the coffee shop so that you can arrive *early*. That way, you can be sure to get a small table (rather than the squashy arm chairs), you won't be all red faced and out of breath, and your date has to find you, (rather than the other way around). They'll turn up, and there you'll be, looking all lovely and relaxed. Remember to take a book with you to read whilst you wait, that way you won't sit there nervously biting your nails or getting impatient, and it'll also give your potential something to talk about if they're struggling.

"What's that you're reading?" they'll ask.

"Oh, just a novel," you'll reply. *"The Truth About This Charming Man.* By Peter Jones. It's very funny. Have you read it?"

What to do when they arrive

When your date arrives – depending on your take on traditional gender roles – it might not be a bad idea to offer to get them a drink. This'll give them the opportunity to settle down and relax, and check out your book. Pay for the drinks, but don't make a big deal out of it. It's only coffee. If they try to offer you money brush it away with a smile and a comment such as "you can get the next one."

By the way, it goes without saying that you don't have to drink coffee – in many ways it's better to drink hot chocolate. Especially if it's cold outside. Hot chocolate is one of those gorgeous smells that most people associate with being warm and cosy, which we can use to your advantage. Studies show that if you give someone a warm pleasant drink – such as hot chocolate – they report the 'drink giver' as 'nicer' than someone who might hand them a more neutral beverage. Why? Because whilst our brains are marvellous things they're not particularly good at attributing feelings correctly when several things are happening at once. It's as if the brain says. "Hot chocolate eh? Hot chocolate makes me feel nice. I'm feeling nice. You're here whilst I'm feeling nice. Therefore, you must be nice too." And this'll work whether your date is the one drinking the hot chocolate, or just smelling yours.

The general ambience of the coffee shop will have the same effect too. If it's a nice place with a relaxed comfortable vibe, in the mind of your potential you'll be credited – at least in part – with having a "relaxed comfortable vibe". But, pick a less than satisfactory coffee venue and *you too* will become 'less than satisfactory'. Another good reason to find a coffee place you like long before you arrange a meet-up.

When it comes to food, avoid eating anything more than a relatively small cake or cookie. You're meeting for coffee. Don't start ordering lunch. For one thing, it's hard to be attractive when you're shovelling food into your gob. Let's establish a good first impression before you go ordering the extra saucy spaghetti meatballs for two.

Finally, keep your mobile phone in your pocket or bag, preferably on silent. DON'T put it on the table. DON'T answer it. Check it when YOU go to the loo (*not* when *they* do – they might come back early).

Do they like you?

Traditional dating advice books and pick-up guides are full of advice on how to tell if a date is going well. They'll tell you to examine your potential's body language and look for 'indicators of interest' such as 'mirroring' (where the other person subconsciously starts to mirror your actions), playing with a necklace, touching their face or neck, licking their lips, baring their palms, dangling a shoe off of one foot or finding an excuse to touch your upper arm or hands.

Personally, I'm usually too busy trying not to put my elbow in the puddle of hot chocolate I created when I spilt my drink, worrying about whether I have foam on my upper lip, and paying attention to what my potential is saying over the deafening roar of that bloody milk frothing machine. I don't have enough mental capacity to keep a look out for such clues. And besides, I truly believe that in your heart of hearts you know whether something is going well or not. But here's how to check:

If the coffee place has public toilets excuse yourself at a convenient juncture, and when you have some privacy, stare into the mirror and ask yourself the following question.

DO YOU STILL LIKE THEM?

Now be honest with yourself here. The questions *isn't* do you *want* to like them?, or do they like *you?* – we're not interested in the answers to either of those questions, because – odd though it may seem – the answers aren't actually useful. What we *do* need to know is how *you* feel about *them*.

If the answer to the above question is 'no' then well done you. I'm proud of you. You gave it your best shot, and achieved what you set out to do – which was to establish whether or not the two of you have a future, and hard though it may be to admit it, you haven't.

Don't despair. Today was good practice. Next time – and *there will be a next time* – will go even better. Right now, though, it's time to go back to your table, finish up your coffee, and leave for that 'appointment' you've just remembered.

If, on the other hand, the answer to the above is 'yes – you do still like them' then here's a follow up question:

DO YOU WANT TO SEE THEM AGAIN?

If the answer is 'I'm not sure' – well, that's a tricky one. Personal experience has led me to believe 'I'm not sure' is just a 'no' in disguise, but you can easily find out. Take a coin, and flip it. Whilst it's still in the air there will be a moment when you secretly hope it's going to come down one way or the other – whatever you're secretly hoping for, that's your answer.

If the answer's 'yes – you'd like to see them again', then take it from me, it's going well. Really well. And it's time for you to move on up to the next phase.

Phase Four: Arranging a 'First Date'

So, 'coffee' is going well – at least from our perspective it is, and, for now, that's all that really matters. Time to see if they feel the same way by 'arranging' a 'first date'.

Now I know what you're thinking. "But I thought we didn't *do* first dates!" Did I say that? Did I actually use those words? What I said was that I hate *traditional* first dates with all the nervous anticipation and nonsense that goes with it – but things have changed. You're in the company of someone you're getting on with swimmingly. The dynamics are completely different. Now, *right now,* whilst you're getting on so well, is actually the perfect opportunity to embark on a 'first date'. And so long as you've actually picked a coffee venue that's within walking distance of a nice pub, or bar, or restaurant, this is actually a possibility.

So what next?

Well, what you *don't* do is swagger back to the table and suggest to your potential that you "embark on a first date". Neither do you mention that you've already checked out three nearby first date venues, all the time brimming with a level of smugness that is just crying out for a slap. You definitely do not do that.

Instead, 'casually' suggest going for a drink. Or a bite to eat. And do it with a smile. Like this:

"Hey, how about we go get a proper drink? There's a nice pub round the corner. It's kind of a couples place but we could pretend we've known each other for ages."

Or: "Are you peckish? There's a lovely little pizza place just over the river? It's one of my favourite places actually and I'd love to show it to you."

Or. "Do you like French food? I walked past this French bar on the way here and noticed they do mussels in wine."

Notice that there's no mention of 'coffee' turning into a 'first date', and that's exactly how it should be. Things are just naturally leading to other things. Easy, and casual. Easy and casual.

Notice too, that we didn't offer a choice. Pick the one *you* would most like to do and then offer it up for consideration. We don't want to get into a discussion that we could do A, or maybe B, or there's always C. That's way too complicated.

Personally, my preference is to suggest 'drinks' – mainly because the nearby pub has three large, squishy leather sofas. Should we be lucky enough to grab one of them, then together with a bottle of wine, an ice bucket and two large glasses, I *already know* it'll be a fabulous first date. And after the drinks there's always the pizza place or, well, more drinks! But we're getting ahead of ourselves. What needs to happen first is for you to pop the question, and wait for one of three possible answers…

1) They say yes! In which case, finish your coffee, grab your coat, and proceed to Phase Five!

2) They say 'they'd love to', and then follow it swiftly with a 'but', and a reason why they can't – usually that they have other plans. This is the most likely outcome. After all, this was only supposed to be 'coffee'. Nothing was mentioned about doing anything afterwards (and let's just be very clear on this point, that's exactly how it should be. Don't go changing the game plan for subsequent 'coffee' appointments. This works. Stick with it). The thing to do at this point is to smile, and say something like, "no worries – another time maybe." Then leave it at that (unless they produce an appointment diary). As you're leaving the coffee shop, casually ask for their number and offer yours, You'll need it tomorrow.

3) They squirm uncomfortably, change the subject, disappear to the loos, or say something that's basically long-hand for 'no thanks'. This is the worst case scenario, and pretty much means that the feelings you have for your potential aren't mutual. There's a chance of course that they're just not that into drinking, or eating, and that they might go for one of your alternative first date options – it's up to you whether you decide to suggest something else – but it's a long

shot. The reality is it hasn't worked out. What you need to do now is gather up your things, wish them all the best, and get out of there as soon as you can. Try not to beat yourself up – you got this far, and you'll get this far again, but this one, isn't *the one*.

Let's recap on how the coffee / first date thing should work.

STOP! ACTION POINT!

The Coffee Date

The basics:

- Make yourself reminders.
- Send a reminder to your potential.
- Your wardrobe; Make an effort, but not so much that it looks like you have.
- Counter nerves by practicing the date in your head.
- Arrive early, take a book, consider hot chocolate.

They arrive:

- Offer them a drink.
- Avoid meals.
- Phone on silent, hidden away.

Is it going well? Ask yourself:

- Do you still like them?
- Do you want to see them again?

If YES, suggest going for a drink or a meal, and either:

- Proceed to 'first date' location.
- Agree to do it another time (get a number).

Phase Four (b): Arranging a 'Second Date'

The only way you should find yourself at Phase 4b, is if your coffee date went well, but the 'surprise first date' wasn't convenient for your potential, but they did express some sort of desire to see you again.

In a sense you've stepped backwards. Back to the world of traditional dating expectations, where 'dates' are scary, and pre-arranged.

You've also lost some ground here. Your potential now has time to weigh-up how they feel about you, and do so in the light of whatever else is going on in their life. Perhaps they've received an intriguing message from someone else who's equally, if not better looking, and also competing for their attentions. Or perhaps they've just had a run in with their ex, and now relationships – and therefore you – don't seem anywhere near as appealing as they did when the two of you were sharing coffee.

For this reason, it's very important to strike whilst the iron's still relatively warm and arrange another meet-up as soon as you possibly can. The day after your initial 'coffee date' call them[41], tell them what a great time you had, and ask them whether they'd like to meet-up *later in the week*.

Where to meet

As before, it's best to have a couple of date suggestions ready, thereby avoiding that 'what would you like to do' conversation. They don't have to be completely new suggestions – you could easily use the same restaurants or bars you had prepared at Phase Four – but there's also a school of thought that suggests you should go for something more exciting.

---

[41] Calling is best, text messaging is second best, sending an email would be third. Avoid using the dating site if you can.

Research suggests that any activity that increases the heart rate – either due to physical exertion, or exhilaration – is likely to speed up that rapport building process.

It's that brain attribution thing again. The brain says, "My heart seems to be beating unusually fast. People I like make my heart beat faster. You're here. Therefore, I must like you."

It sounds like nonsense but it goes some way to explaining a rather successful date I had many years ago with a fabulously beautiful lady who, back then, I considered way out of my league. For complicated reasons that I'm not getting into we found ourselves walking along Southend Pier.

Southend Pier, in case you're unfamiliar with it, is allegedly the longest 'pleasure pier' in the world[42]. It's had a chequered history. Every couple of years a boat manages to collide with it, or someone sets it alight, and yet it's still standing. I can look out of my window right now and, yes, there it is. A fine monument to British Engineering.

That's not how it seems when you're up close and personal, walking its length on what appear to be rotting planks of wood, the cold brown murky water clearly visible between the huge gaps. Every step you take is another moment when you might disappear down a hole of your own making, followed by bits of disintegrating timber. After a while, you start looking over your shoulder back towards the shore, just to check how far it is should you have to swim.

These were the thoughts going through the head of my companion, who was absolutely certain that her three-inch heels were sinking into the wood beneath our feet, as she held on to my arm for dear life.

But a curious thing happened when we got to the end of the pier. She still had hold of my arm, and she didn't let go.

Personally, whilst I like the idea, there aren't that many piers in Central London that offer that sense of impending doom and the viewing gallery of Tower Bridge just isn't scary enough. But if you're

---

[42] Which presumably means there are far longer, less pleasurable piers.

a bit of a thrill seeker and you can think of a venue that might just work – give it a go, and let me know how it works out.

I usually suggest meeting at the same coffee venue where we met before, but this time make it clear that we'll be moving on elsewhere. This way, my date doesn't have to find anywhere new, and we're essentially picking up from where we left off, which is exactly how I want it to feel.

Re-framing the date

There is no getting away from it, though. This time, you really are going on a 'first date'. Which is why, if the subject of 'first dates' gets raised, I usually suggest calling this the *'second date'*.

"Nobody likes first dates," I say, "first dates are scary and awkward. Second dates are much more fun. All sorts of exciting things can happen on a second date. Let's have our second date now, and save our first date for another occasion."

In psychological terms this is called 're-framing'. Have you ever noticed how a picture can look entirely different if you change its frame – it's not just pictures that can be re-framed.

This always goes down well. If you do it right it can become an in-joke between the two of you, and in-jokes are a *powerful* way of creating rapport. Once, as we sat together on a particularly squishy sofa, I leant forward and put my hand on my date's knee – she raised an eyebrow.

"That's a little forward for a first-date," she said.

"But not for a second date," I countered, and moved in a little closer.

Let's get you arranging that 'second' date.

STOP! ACTION POINT!

Arrange The 'Second' Date

- Phone the day after your coffee date.
- Suggest meeting up later in the week.
- Consider starting at the same coffee location...

...before you move on to...
a) a great bar or restaurant, or
b) something more exhilarating.

- Reframe this date. It's a 'second' date, not the first.

Phase Five: The 'First/Second' date

Let's recap how you got here: You were either drinking coffee a few moments earlier and suggested popping over the road for a drink or a bite to eat – *or* having been for coffee a couple of days ago you suggested meeting up *today*.

Well, congratulations. For some of you, you're only pages away from being able to put down this book – maybe forever – pausing only briefly to leave me a five star review on a website of your choice, and publicly declaring me something of a demi-god amongst dating advice givers.

Do this phase right and you'll be embarking upon a new relationship and all the excitement that that entails... *if* your date is a success.

And why shouldn't it be a success?

Seriously. The two of you got this far – one of you picked the other from shed-loads of available potentials, you've exchanged several messages, maybe a phone call, met each other in person, had coffee together, and successfully arranged a date. It's all been good. And with my help *this* will feel like the best date you've ever been on.

What to talk about

Unless you're leaping off objects with a bungee cord attached to your ankles, scaling walls, or something equally dangerous, chances are you're going to be doing a lot of talking, and, generally speaking, talking is good.

When I was a kid, I used to invite girls to the pictures. We'd walk to the cinema in near silence, sit through the film in silence, and finally we'd walk home and barely exchange a word. *None* of those dates ever amounted to anything. If anyone ever invents time travel I'm going back in time to give my younger self a stern talking to. Here's what I'm going to tell him: Relationships are forged, built and sustained on communication and intimacy, in equal measure. It's not enough to be in the same physical location if you never open your mouth.

Having messed up the space time continuum I'd leap forward to my early twenties, where I'd track down the lanky long-haired version of myself who'd become convinced that the fastest way to get a girl to like him was to ask her a LOT of questions. I'd remind *him* that communication is a two way street. You have to give as much as you get. Your date should learn as much about you as you're learning about them.

And finally, just to be sure that I'd caused a time paradox of sci-fi movie proportions, I'd pop in on thirty-something Jonesy – the *idiot* who'd decided that shutting up, listening and nodding was a sure-fire way to dating success. I'd punch him in the face.

None of these approaches work.

What *does work* is an equal exchange of steadily more and more personal information when both parties feel ready and comfortable[43]. And one way to do this is by turning it into a game.

The question game

The rules are simple: Each person takes it in turn to ask the other person *any* question they like, and the other person *has to* give them a truthful answer.

The wonderful thing about the question game is that it:

- Prevents either party from hogging the conversation (useful if you are – or you're dating – a bit of a chatterbox).
- The questions always start pretty tame and get steadily more intimate as people get braver, and enjoy it more.
- There's a delicious frisson of excitement as both players wonder just how intimate the next question will be.

And here are some secret tips, that'll help make the game work better:

---

[43] Needless to say, scientists have actually researched this. I'm beginning to wonder how one volunteers for these kind of studies. It might be a good way to meet people.

Introduce the game as though it's your idea and you just made it up. "Hey, I've got an idea…"

Make sure *you* start, and do so with a really tame question: "What's your favourite place in the whole wide world?"

Keep nudging the intimacy level upwards, but in small incremental steps.

Steer clear of questions about regret, or sadness, or anything that would make the other player imagine those scenarios. Ask about their happiest moments, and what gets them excited. You want to raise their heart beat if you can.

Stick rigidly to taking it in turns! There will come a moment when your date will want to ask a follow up question to the one they've just asked, but honestly, this rule makes it much more fun.

If the other person keeps using your questions (rather than thinking of their own) introduce a rule to prevent that.

I almost didn't add this tip, but what the hell – if things are going really, really *really* well (let's say you've been playing this for a couple of hours and it feels like the two of you are inside your own private little bubble), hit them with this question; "can I kiss you?"[44]

Other Rapport Building Tips

The question game works because it accelerates the natural rapport-building process. In fact, much of what we've discussed in the past few pages is about creating an environment where you and your potential find it easy to connect and develop that 'feels like I've known you my whole damn life' moment.

Another 'rapport-building' tool in my dating toolbox is 'palmistry'. There are two types of palmistry in the world; Chiromancy and Chirology. The former is all about fortune telling, the latter is more about how the shape of someone's hand and how the lines on the palm and fingers can sometimes be an indicator of certain personality traits. Whilst the former can be a little spooky

---

[44] Yes, I've done this. Yes, it works. Ladies you might want to change the question to "would you like to kiss me?"

(especially, one supposes, if you turn out to be accurate), the latter is a fantastic opportunity to touch the other person's hand, get really close together so that you can both see those faint little 'marriage lines' on the little finger, or the passion line at the base of the thumb, and discuss some very personal topics. Ten minutes of googling the topic on the internet will turn you into something of a palm-reading expert and increase your chances of a third or fourth date.

Nicknames, too, build rapport. I have a friend who makes sure she issues her man-of-the-moment with a cute nick name as soon as she can, to cement the relationship.

There are countless other rapport-building tricks and games. *Google* some.

Setting up the next date

Whilst you're finding out about each other, be on the lookout for any nuggets of information that you can squirrel away and use for the basis of a 'second/third date'. If nothing's forthcoming ask them (perhaps during the question game) what their favourite food is. Indian? Chinese? Italian? Bratislavan? Bingo. Now you have restaurant options.

Alternatively, talk about one of your interests and wait for the golden phrase 'I'd love to do that' or something similar. Are you a bit of a chef? Talk about that, and describe your signature dish in mouth-watering detail. When they tell you that sounds absolutely delicious make a mental note.

Sex?

Back in my teens, twenties, and – let's be honest – even my thirties, I never had to worry about whether or not I should have sex on a first date. It was never, *ever*, going to happen. But that was *before*. Before Kate got her hands on me. Before numerous image makeovers. Before internet dating. Before I started adopting the strategies discussed in this book. Before I worked out who I am! Since then, well, let's just say things have changed somewhat.

This is where I dearly wish I could move the spotlight away from me and show you some nice graphs and charts that a bespectacled scientist or statistician somewhere has produced – results of detailed study researchers performed into those people who ended up having sex on a first date, and how it affected the relationship going forwards. But I can't. I only have my own experience to go on. A less-than-statistical sample of one.

That said, this is a subject that I feel quite strongly about, and without going into too much detail, I can honestly say that (in my experience) if you want to increase your chances of making it past *Phase Five*, if you want to avoid your dating exploits becoming more than occasional one-night-stands, when it comes to 'sex on the first date' (even though we've reframed this the second date) *don't do it*.

It's easy for me to say this now – you might even be nodding your head in agreement – but after the coffee, the drinks, the question game, a second bottle of wine, some palm reading, and the "would you like to kiss me" moment – the rapport between you might be so strong that *not* going back to their place (or yours) for 'coffee' (and this time by coffee I mean anything but) will seem like utter madness.

But resist you must.

Even if the conversation has turned incredibly intimate. Even if there's barely enough room between you for a single Kleenex tissue.

Even if the other person is begging you to take them home (yes, this could happen)…

Don't.

It's far better to be sitting on that train, trundling homewards, a stupid grin all over your face, feeling high as a kite on all the hormones and endorphins you've been generating, than to wake up the following morning, in a strange bed, in the cold light of day, with – dare I say it – *regrets*. You know what I'm going to say next don't you.

Yes, it's happened to me.

Worst of all, is when those regrets aren't actually yours, but the other person's. There's nothing more heartbreaking than spending a magical first night with someone only to have them tell you in the morning, either in words or by their body language, that they're having second thoughts, that the 'magical' time you spent together might have been a mistake, or the product of too much alcohol. You thought all those ignored messages, those failed dates, those scammers, spammers, liars and Lotharios were cruel? You ain't experienced anything yet!

I'm here to tell you that the only way to avoid this level of heartache is to prevent it from happening in the first place. From now on you must abide by the ninth and possibly most important rule of dating.

DATING GOLDEN RULE #9:
NEVER EVER SLEEP WITH SOMEONE
ON THE FIRST DATE
(EVEN IF YOU'VE REFRAMED IT AS THE SECOND DATE)

Fortunately, so long as your refusal to jump into bed doesn't come across as some sort of rejection (more on that in a second) there are major upsides to this level of abstention.

Firstly, when you and your potential wake up tomorrow – not just in separate beds, but separate parts of the country – any hangover you and your potential might have will be correctly attributed to the alcohol, *not you*. Neither one of you will be sheepishly looking at the other person and wondering whether you'd have done what you did had you been stone cold sober. Those awful words "maybe this is all moving a little too fast" will never be uttered.

Instead, as your hangovers wear off, the lovely butterfly feeling you and your potential share in the pit of your collective stomachs will linger on. The two of you will keep thinking back to the magic of the evening, instead of the nightmare of the morning.

Your polite refusal to jump into the sack will, to most people, come across as a good thing – even if they're disappointed[45]. After all, you're clearly a picky person. You *don't* go to bed with just anyone. In the mind of your potential this raises your social value, and they'll realise – subconsciously if not consciously – that it raises theirs too when the deed finally takes place. Put simply, you'll be even more attractive than you were.

Do this right and your potential should definitely want to see you again! More than that, deciding on your second/third date location might amount to nothing more than 'your place or mine' (you cheeky thing) – but for now let's make sure you know how to gently back out of sex-on-the-first-date without screwing everything up.

Turning Down Sex

The best way to avoid sex on the 'first' date is to not mention it in the first place! But should the other person shuffle forwards in their seat and whisper in your ear that they want you to take them home, here's how to back out without causing rejection.

Explain, gently, that you never ever have sex on a first date – especially if the other person's been drinking. You want to be sure that it's their passion talking, not the wine. Always, *always* smile as you say this. Some sort of physical contact – holding hands for instance – works too. You want them to know that you really like them, that you *do* want to have sex with them – just not right now. Then kiss them.

---

[45] I'll go as far to say that if you meet someone who reacts badly to your refusal to sleep with them on a first date, they're probably the sort of person you should steer clear of. Well done. You've just saved yourself from a world of heartache and pain.

Alternatively, you could *lie*.

There's the ever popular 'my mother's staying with me' ploy. Downside; they may assume by mother, you mean the spouse you somehow failed to mention. Or they might simply suggest you go to their place.

You could tell them you're not going home, but instead you're stopping with a friend for whatever reason takes your fancy. Downside; they'll suggest you cancel it, and later (probably when you introduce them to aforementioned friend) that lie will come back and bite you in the backside.

There's always, 'I'd love to but have work tomorrow' – but this merely leads to a "what time?" or "me too, I can be up and out first thing" response.

Each of these lies also negate the final benefit of politely refusing their advances – you won't be seen as someone who's choosy, you'll be seen as someone who isn't prepared to make a few inconvenient sacrifices. They'll feel that you don't particularly think they're worth the effort. Consequently, you'll become *less* attractive.

Stick with the 'truth' – or at least the version I've presented you with. You'll not go far wrong.

Incidentally, it occurs to me now that some of you might be assuming I'm using a broad definition of sex that includes kissing, touching, or any kind of physical contact. I'm not. I definitely mean *sex*. If your post-drink romantic walk along the Thames turns into a passionate snog under Tower Bridge, good for you. Just make sure that's where the evening ends.

And one final thought, just like the 'coffee' meet-up, and the first / second date, you want your 'first time' together to appear carefree, romantic, and super sexy – and, by now, I'm sure you realise that this level of spontaneity requires careful planning! We'll cover that in the next section but for now let's recap Phase Five.

STOP! ACTION POINT!

The 'First/Second' Date

Relationships are forged, built and sustained on communication and intimacy, in equal measure. Build rapport with...
- The question game.
- Nicknames.
- Palmistry, handwriting analysis, whatever works for you.

When it comes to sex on the first date...

a) Don't raise the subject!

b) Don't make up phony reasons why it's not possible.

c) Politely, sincerely, and gently back out, whilst smiling and maintaining physical contact.

d) Remember the ninth golden rule:

DATING GOLDEN RULE #9:
NEVER EVER SLEEP WITH SOMEONE
ON THE FIRST DATE
(EVEN IF YOU'VE REFRAMED IT AS THE SECOND DATE)

Phase Six: The Morning After

So, I'm assuming that last night was a huge success – and, depending just how huge, this might be a totally irrelevant section, but just to be sure let's cover some basics.

Make contact

If you haven't already you *must* make contact with your potential. Send them a short message telling them how much you enjoyed the evening. If you gave them a nickname, use it. If you established any other in-jokes use those. Do whatever's necessary to remind the other person what a fabulous time the two of you had together. Don't go sending cards or flowers – you haven't time[46] – you need to strike now whilst the iron's still glowing. Send a message.

Arrange to see each other again

Once they've replied to your message, jump right in and arrange your next meet-up. Avoid the phrase, "Would you like to meet up again?" – this presupposes that there might be some doubt in the matter. Of course they want to see you again! And until anything is said to the contrary this is what you're going to believe.

As before, suggest a date and a venue. Having spent an evening grilling them for personal information it should be significantly easier to think of something appropriate, and with the power of *Google* at your fingertips it should take no more than five minutes to find a highly recommended Bratislavan restaurant.

Alternatively, invite them over to your place and cook them that signature dish you spent so long telling them about. Personally, that's what I would do. And, it goes without saying, that, as well as picking a dish that can be made in advance and heated up when

---

[46] Plus it's a little intense!

necessary, I would have a really good tidy up, *including* the bedroom. You know, just in case.

Everybody's different, though, and we're entering territory that's increasingly hard to advise on because so much depends on you, your potential, and how the two of you are together. But whatever you decide to do it's important to open up all lines of communication.

Stay in contact

Having arranged the next date there's no need to stop messaging each other. I'm a firm believer that the invention of the mobile phone and text messaging has done more for romance than online dating websites ever could. How frequently you bat messages back and forth, and how flirty those messages are is, of course, down to you – both of you – but odds are if you want to keep some of the magic from that first date alive, frequent communication is the way to go.

Let's recap.

STOP! ACTION POINT!

The Morning After.

- Make contact!
- Arrange the next meet-up. Either:

a) Use information gleaned from last night (things they expressed an interest in) to create a date, or...

b) Invite them to an event you were 'already' going to (i.e. an interest you have, that they share).

- Stay in contact.

Phases Seven Onwards

You've made it. To date number two. Three. Whatever you decided it was. I dunno, I've lost count. The point is, though, that in a few short pages you've gone from finding someone to regular dating. Well done you. You're building the basis of a new relationship. Which, I'm afraid, means it's almost time for you and I to part company. This is a book about dating, not relationships. From here on you're on your own.

That said, if it doesn't work out, you can pick this book up again, rewind to wherever you feel's necessary and we can start over. And next time, if there needs to be a next time, you'll be all the better for the practice.

Part 3

"Everything will be all right in the end.
If it's not all right, it's not the end."

DEFENCE AGAINST DISILLUSIONMENT

So. You're finally dating. Which is great news. Really, *really* great. It pains me then to be the one to tell you that, at some point... you're going to be disappointed. I once heard it said that to be disillusioned you first have to be under an illusion, and if ever this were true, it's definitely true of dating.

When that awful day arrives some will tell you that your dating exploits failed because "people aren't perfect", or that "the world we live in isn't perfect", which suggests that we are flawed people living in a flawed world. There are at least two responses to this: Live with it, or fix it!

I just can't help myself. Call it a gift, but if I can see how something – *anything* – can be engineered to work better then before you can say "excuse me but that's my life you're messing with" I'm in there, tinkering about, fixing stuff. In my head a voice is telling me that if I could fix *everything*, or maybe just *most things*, then the whole world would run a lot more smoothly! But whilst that might be true, often the easiest things to fix are expectations.

In a way that's what this book has been about: Showing you how the world of dating actually works – rather than how it *should* work – then helping you to figure out how to make it work for you.

This last chapter then ties up a few loose ends, realigns the odd expectation, stamps out a few more occurrences of the word *should* from your vocabulary, and rids you of the *illusion* once and for all.

Beware 'Perfect People'

Every now and then you're going to meet someone who seems... *perfect*.

They're going to be funny. They're going to be smart. They're going to be gorgeous. They're going to be just what you've been looking for your whole life, or what you *should* have been looking for your whole life, or what you decided to start looking for ten minutes ago.

All your usual background checks will confirm what you already know. Your dating site match score will somehow be over 100 per cent. *Facebook* will keep asking whether the two of you know each other. *Twitter* will recommend you follow each other to the ends of the earth.

Maybe the two of you will meet for coffee. Maybe you'll make it to that first / second date. Maybe you'll even get as far as the bedroom. And then...

Oh dear.

Suddenly, what seems so obvious to *you* has somehow eluded them entirely. That future that destiny had so clearly mapped out for the two of you, seems less clear to them.

Your words will start to fall on deaf ears. Your charm will miss its mark. Nothing you do or say will make any difference. And that 'happy ever after' you were *so sure* was just around the corner will seem more elusive than ever before.

There are many, many relationship books and seduction guides that talk about courtship dynamics – how to move from attraction, through comfort building, and towards the 'end-game' – but even if you've done *everything* this book, the companion guide, and all the other books out there have told you to do, every now and then you're *still* going to meet people who somehow just don't get how extraordinarily lovely you are.

And here's the thing: why would you want to be with someone like that?

People who don't message you back. People who flake on you halfway through a message exchange. People who stand you up on dates, or never contact you again after date number one. No matter how gorgeous they might be, *they're not worth your effort.*

Let's make it the final rule.

DATING GOLDEN RULE #10:
IF YOU MEET SOMEONE SO STUPID
THAT THEY CAN'T SEE HOW LOVELY YOU ARE
THEY'RE NOT WORTH YOUR ATTENTION.
MOVE ON.

Beware 'Happy Ever After'

Human beings are complicated creatures. We barely understand ourselves, let alone each other, and whilst people like me spend much of our time dreaming up boy-meets-girl stories that inevitably finish up with an implied "and they all lived happily ever after", back in the real world things work somewhat differently. Put simply, whilst everyone wants a happy ever after, we don't necessarily want the *same* happy ever after.

Back at the start of this book we spent some time figuring out just what it is you want. That strategy alone will save you days, perhaps even weeks, of heartache. But you can save yourself even more pain and frustration by doing the same for everyone you meet – figuring out what it is *they're* after – and determining whether your end-games are compatible.

For instance, it's easy to assume that *most* people you'll encounter in the dating community must be looking for a partner whom they can wine, dine, and if things go well, ultimately settle down with – but actually that's less likely than you'd think. *Far* less likely.

Here are four types of people who might have written an entirely different ending for Cinders and Prince Charming, given half a chance.

The Online Flirt

There's a growing number of people, both men and women, for whom *online* dating *is* the Happy Ever After. They get to experience the 'thrill' of the chase, the window shopping, the flirting, and they have absolutely no intentions whatsoever of meeting anyone in real life. One imagines that, for them, online dating must be considerably easier. They can say what they like, use stolen pictures, make up an entire alter ego – and so long as they're cautious they'll never be found out, either by you or their spouse. Effectively, they've created an online fantasy-reality game of which you are just a character. To them, you're not actually real.

For me, these are the most frustrating 'daters' you're likely to come across. But stick to the advice earlier in the book (check the pictures, don't exchange too many messages, arrange coffee as soon as you can) and you should be able to flush them out pretty quickly.

Let's talk about those folk who *are* prepared to meet you.

Beware Serial Daters

I discovered an interesting phenomenon in recent years. I met not one, but two ladies (at separate times, I hasten to add), who enjoyed the excitement of dating so much that they were unwilling to do anything else. Suggest an evening in a swanky wine bar somewhere in the West End and they'd drop whatever they were doing, don a little black number, some killer heels, and meet you at the bar a few hours later. Suggest they might like to come over for dinner, or go away for the weekend, or share a pizza, curl up on the sofa and watch a DVD together – or anything else that looked suspiciously like, well, an actual relationship – and they became inexplicably 'busy'.

Our evenings would always go well. The conversation, much like the wine, would flow effortlessly. We'd move closer and closer and closer together until the air would almost crackle with the level of intimacy between us. We'd be that couple in the corner you'd wish would get a room. And then someone would ring a bell for last orders, we'd gather up our coats, my date would hail a cab, and I'd be left standing by the side of the road, kisses and promises hanging in the air where she'd stood, wondering where I'd gone wrong. It took me a while to realise that I *hadn't*. From my dates' perspective, I was the perfect man. Someone who allowed them to be a 'serial dater' – a strange breed of person who's happiest bouncing between Phases Five and Six.

I like dates. They're fun, in the same way that a cross country train journey down to Devon or Cornwall can be fun. But for me, part of that fun is knowing I'm en-route to somewhere nice. It would have to be an exceptionally nice train for me to declare it 'the destination' and stay there for any length of time. But everyone's different. And one of the lessons I've learnt in life is that there is no 'normal'. It's an illusion. Especially when it comes to relationships.

The only way to deal with a serial dater (or indeed anyone who has relationship ideals that are fundamentally different from your own) is either to practice acceptance (by which I mean come to terms with the fact that this is all that's on offer), or move on. As acceptance probably isn't an option (if it were then you wouldn't be viewing it as a problem), that leaves you with 'moving on', which can be exceptionally hard to do.

After all the effort you've put in, the thought of starting over will feel nauseating, especially when this person is *almost* perfect, were it not for their annoying serial dating tendencies. It's at this point many people wonder if there's a viable third option; i.e. *change them*. Bend the other person to your will. Force, manipulate, seduce, blackmail – whatever it takes to *make* them into what you want. As someone who's been on the receiving end of all those strategies let me be the first to tell you this never, ever, works.

Accept or move on. Those are your only options.

The Hot Affair

According to research[47], roughly half of all men <u>and</u> women admit to having had some sort of affair during their lifetime, and of those, at least a third claim to be happily married[48]. In other words, if you happen to subscribe to the popular belief that affairs are a symptom of an unhappy union, this could be cause to revisit that assumption. Especially when I tell you that the research goes on to reveal that around <u>seventy</u> per cent of all men AND women admitted that they *would* cheat on their partner if there was absolutely no chance they would get caught. Ethics aside, we are not the monogamous species many would like to think that we are.

---

[47] Links to all the research and scientific papers referenced in this book can be found on the website.
[48] Actually the statistic is 56 percent of men and 34 percent of women (who have affairs) claim to be happily married.

So, putting aside your personal thoughts on the subject, during the course of your dating exploits you're statistically *very* likely to meet people who are not only already in a relationship, but have absolutely no intention of giving it up for you, regardless of how fabulous you may be.

Some people just enjoy having affairs.

Now, being the lovely non-judgmental person that you are, you're probably thinking "that's fine, Peter, but why can't those people cheat with *each other* – stick to those niche dating websites for 'naughty people' – and give us loyal, monogamous people a wide berth?" If only life were that simple. If only the 'naughty' websites were that good. And if only you weren't so attractive! But life isn't simple, most of *those* websites are pretty poor, and you're looking particularly gorgeous today. Hence the subterfuge.

Speaking personally, it's not the desire for an 'affair' that bothers me, it's the dishonesty. And I'm not alone. Enter a new breed of folks who prefer their monogamy with a side order. Those for whom the term 'relationship' might include the odd visitor – other than you I mean – to their bedroom.

Non-Monogamists

Non-monogamy is on the increase. You've probably heard of 'open' marriages (where a husband and wife have agreed that they can continue to date others), but there are also those who identify themselves as 'polyamorous' (folk who believe it's entirely possible to have simultaneous multiple loving relationships). There are those less lovey-dovey, but still quite chummy, individuals who prefer to seek out what I recently heard described as 'pillow friends' (where friendship might include more than a peck on the cheek). And, finally, there are the ever-so-slightly-scary 'swingers' and 'wife swappers' who still believe in one-true-love, possibly stood in a church and said some vows to that effect, but also enjoy parties that involve throwing your car keys into a bowl.

These types of non-monogamous relationships are more common than ever, or at least, they're more *visible* than ever, forcing some dating sites to replace the term 'single' with 'available' – even

Facebook has an 'open relationship' option. In my mind, such folk are amongst the pioneers of human evolution. They're experimenting and challenging the social norms. Re-defining the 'relationship'. Taking our ability to manage complex human interactions and propelling us towards new levels of acceptance, honesty and openness, and how can that possibly be a bad thing? If you thought that society's current 'meet-someone, fall-in-love, live-happily-ever-after' model is how it's always been, you're very much mistaken. As a species we've reinvented 'relationships' many, many times in our collective history. In a hundred years from now I have no doubt that today's views on how people meet, and what they get up to when they do, will seem outmoded in the extreme.

But that's the future. And, right now, it isn't for everybody.

Some people, perhaps even most people, wouldn't be able to cope with the idea of their partner, or themselves, 'seeing' more than one person. Many would go as far to say it's 'wrong' or immoral. Sadly, we're not at that stage where a non-monogamist can be completely 'out' without the world doing anything more judgmental than giving a shrug of its collective shoulders. Which means that right now maybe the non-monogamous ideal doesn't quite work in practice, and perhaps it might not be the first thing, or even the second, that gets mentioned on a dating profile. That's not necessarily subterfuge or dishonesty. It's just the way of the world. But it's worth keeping in mind that there's a good possibility that the next person you find yourself getting cosy with on a first date, could easily have someone at home who not only *knows* where they are, but might even ask them how it went. If you're not keen to become part of this 'new-age' 'free-love' movement, best to ask a few carefully worded questions on or before your first date.

Beware 'First Time Lucky'

I happened upon a blog recently by a lady who decided to give online dating a go, and thought her experiences might make interesting reading. She signed up to one of the larger free online dating sites, filled out a profile, uploaded some pictures, answered some questions, and immediately got matched with a local fella. They exchanged a few messages, and arranged to meet. For reasons she didn't go into the date didn't go well. She declared her online dating experience a complete disaster, closed her account, and went back to complaining about how she was destined to live out the rest of her life as a lonely spinster, surrounded by cats.

It shouldn't take a self-help author to point out where she went wrong. But I'm going to anyway.

So the date didn't work out; the next one might. So this guy didn't reply to your message; the next one might. So this website doesn't appear to have many nice people on it; the next one might. So online dating websites aren't really working for you; social media or speed dating might.

The truth is, not every idea in this book is going to work, for you, first time. But, I can guarantee you this; try *everything*, more than once, learn from your previous experience, adapt your approach, and something *will* work eventually. "Happy ever after" rarely appears on the first page of a story. Or the second. Or the third. But it's always there. If you keep turning the pages.

YOU STILL HERE?

Good grief! You've made it to the end of the book! And, suddenly, I find myself wondering whether that's a good thing or a bad thing? What a strange and unusual position for an author to find himself in.

Ah – but I can see from your smile that I have no need to worry. Tell me, have you been... *dating?*

Final Remarks

When I was a lad, my grandmother was in the habit of asking whether I had a girlfriend. And, once I'd turned a deep crimson colour and suddenly became very interested in the floor, she'd follow her query with the line, "faint heart never won fair lady."

It took me many years to figure out what she meant. And it took me almost half a lifetime to figure out what actually does win ladies. Fair or otherwise.

Whether you adopt the principals in this book, or create your own, one thing's for sure, it takes *effort*. Some days, that effort will seem almost too much to bear, but if you learn nothing else from this book, know this; *it's totally worth it*. Nothing can compare with that feeling of being connected with another human being. Nothing. Neither should it.

Best wishes

Peter

If You've Enjoyed This Book…

If you've enjoyed what you read and you'd like to 'spread the word', then here are a few ways you can do just that.

Review the book

Positive reviews are always welcome, help others to decide whether or not they should part with their hard earned cash, and in so doing keeps authors like me in business. If you have five minutes, pop back to wherever you bought this book (and/or Amazon) and leave a glowing five star endorsement.

Follow me on Facebook

If you're on *Facebook* feel free to follow me:
facebook.com/*peterjonesauthor*

Follow me on Twitter

If you're more of a *Twitter*er I tweet under the handle @peterjonesauth.

Got a blog or a podcast?

A mention of the book, or a link to *peterjonesauthor.com* would be most appreciated.

If you'd me to write a guest post for your blog, or interview me, just drop me a line.

Tell a friend

And finally, one of the hardest things for any author to achieve is 'word of mouth' recommendations. Next time you find yourself sitting next to someone who's telling you how hard dating is, do them, yourself, and us a favour – tell them about this book!

If you can do any of these things, I'd like to offer you our heartfelt thanks.

And whilst I'm in the 'thanking' mood…

Acknowledgements

In no particular order I'd really like to thank:

To Jules – for her endless wisdom, friendship, and making the really important stuff in my life 'happen' whilst I continue to gamble it all. I couldn't have done this without you.

To Val – for her support, love, and continuing belief in me and my odd choice of career.

To Sarah, Kelly Ann, and the all other readers who loved the first edition of this book and could see ways it might be *even better*.

And to you, dear reader, for continuing to read long after others might have put this book down. How awesome are you? Pretty darn awesome!

Thank you all.

What Should I Read Next?

You know that feeling when you get to the end of a book and you're not quite sure what to read next? Or that maybe the next book on your TBR[49] pile might not be *quite* as good as the one you've just finished?

Yeah. I feel your pain.

But fortunately, I also have the solution!

Why not allow me to entertain you once again with my witty words of wisdom, or – if you're in the mood for fiction – a torrid tale of comic capers?

Simply pop over to my website (web-address below), for links to all my books.

Hope to see you soon!

Peter :-)

www.PeterJonesAuthor.com

---

[49] To Be Read

APPENDIX 1: COMMON TLAS & ABBREVIATIONS

These are some of the more common TLAs (three letter acronyms) and abbreviations you're likely to come across in dating profiles, messages or 'chat' sessions.

2NITE
tonight

420
refers to the use of cannabis

ADN
any day now

AFAIK
as far as I know

AFK
away from keyboard

AKA
also known as

AML
all my love

ASAP
as soon as possible

ASLP
age/sex/location/picture

AWYR
awaiting your reply

B4
before

B4N
bye for now

BAK
back at keyboard

BBL
be back later

BBC
big black cock

BBW
big beautiful woman

BCNU
be seeing you

BDSM
bondage & discipline/domination & submission/sadism & masochism

BEG
big evil grin

BF
boyfriend

BFF
best friends forever

BFFL
best friends for life

BFN
bye for now

BRB
be right back
(as in, "I've got to answer the door" etc)

BS
big smile/bullshit
(that could make for an interesting misunderstanding!)

BTAIM
be that as it may

BTU
back to you

BTW
by the way

BWK
big wet kiss

CBL
come back later

CIO
check it out

CU
see you

CUL
catch you later

CWYL
chat with you later

DDF
drug and disease free

DIKU
do I know you?

DILIGAS
does it look like I give a sh*t?

Div
divorced

DLN
don't leave now

DLTM
don't lie to me

273

DTE
down to earth

EG
evil grin

F/ship
friendship

FAQ
frequently asked questions

FOTCL
falling off the chair laughing

FFS
for f***'s sake

FTF
face to face

FWB
friends with 'benefits'
('benefits' being sex)

FWIW
for what it's worth

FYI
for your information

G2G
got to go

274

GAL
get a life!

GF
girlfriend

GFAK
go fly a kite

GIO
get it over

GL
good luck

GMAB
give me a break!

GSOH
good sense of humour

GTSY
glad to see you

H&K
hug and kisses

HAGN
have a good night

HAK
more hugs and kisses

HB
hurry back

HIG
how's it going?

ICBW
I could be wrong

IDC
I don't care

IDK
I don't know

IDST
I didn't say that!

IGP
I gotta pee

IMHO
in my humble opinion

IMO
in my opinion
(no humility)

IRL
in real life
(e.g. "let's meet IRL")

276

ISO
in search of

J/K
just kidding

JAM
just a minute

JAS
just a second

KIT
keep in touch

KWIM
know what I mean?

L8R
later

LDR
long distance relationship

LJBF
let's just be friends

LGBT
lesbian gay bisexual transgender

LMAO
laughing my arse off

LOL
laugh out loud
(or, very occasionally, 'lots of love'
– but that's actually a mistake made by newbies)

LOLA
laughing out loud again

LTR
long term relationship

M/F
male/female

M4M
man for man

M4MW
man for couple (man & woman)

M4W
man for woman

M8
mate

MILF
An attractive woman of child bearing age, whom – one
supposes – might make very pleasant company.
(ie. a "mother I'd like to f***")

MOTOS
member of the opposite sex

MOTSS
member of the same sex

MRS
meet real soon

MW4M
couple (man & woman) for man

MW4W
couple (man & woman) for woman

MWBRL
more will be revealed later

MYOB
mind your own business

N1
nice one!

N2S
needless to say

ND
non- drinker

NOYB
none of your business

NP
no problem

NRN
no response necessary

NS
non-smoker

NSA
no strings attached (sex)

NTTAWWT
not that there's anything wrong with that

NW
no way!

OBTW
oh, by the way

OIC
oh I see

OMG
oh my God!

OT
off topic

PDA
public display of affection

PLS
please

POV
point of view

PTB
part time boyfriend

PTG
part time girlfriend

R/ship
relationship

RBTL
read(ing) between the lines

ROTFL
rolling on the floor laughing

ROTFLMAO
rolling on the floor laughing my arse off

ROTFLMAOBSST
rolling on the floor, laughing my arse off – but somehow still
typing!

ROTL
rolling on the floor laughing

RUOK
are you okay?

281

SD
social drinker

SOH
sense of humour

SOL
sooner or later

SOMY
sick of me yet?

SS
social smoker

STD
sexually transmitted disease

SWAK
sealed with a kiss

SWALK
sealed with a *loving* kiss

SYS
see you soon

TAFN
that's all for now

TAH
take a hike!

TBDL
to be discussed later

TBR
to be read

TG
transgender

THX
thanks

TIAIL
think I am in love

TLA
three letter acronym

TLC
tender loving care

TMI
too much information

TNTC
too numerous to count

TS
transsexual

TTFN
"ta ta for now"
(bye)

TTYL
talk to you later

TTYS
talk to you soon

TV
transvestite

TX
thanks

TYVM
thank you very much

VGL
very good looking

VM
voicemail

W/E
well endowed

W4M
woman for man

W4MW
woman for couple (man & woman)

W4W
woman for woman

W8
wait!

WIIFM
what's in it for me?

WGTG
well, got to go

WLTM
would like to meet

WRU
who are you?

WTF
what the f***!?

WTGP
want to go private?
(as in; online private 'chat' mode)

WUF
where are you from?

WWJD
what would Jesus do?

WWPD
what would Peter do?
(not always the same as Jesus)

WWTMM
who was that masked man?

WYS
whatever you say

WYSIWYG
what you see is what you get

XOXO
even *more* hugs and kisses

YNK
you never know

YW
you're welcome